Reforming Teacher Education through Accreditation: Telling Our Story

A Joint Project of The American Association of Colleges for Teacher Education

and

The National Council for Accreditation of Teacher Education

NATIONAL COUNCIL FOR ACCREDITATION
OF TEACHER EDUCATION
2010 Massachusetts Avenue, NW, Suite 500
Washington, DC 20036
1.202.466.7496
www.ncate.org

Library of Congress
Cataloging-in-Publication Data

Reforming teacher education through
accreditation: telling our story/edited by Boyce C.
Williams.

    p.   cm.
    ISBN 0-966-56870-2
    1. Teachers colleges.
  2. Teachers colleges–Accreditation.
I. Williams, Boyce C. II. National Council
for Accreditation of Teacher Education.
III. American Association of Colleges for
Teacher Education.

2000   98-067317
                       CIP

Boyce C. Williams, Editor

Special thanks are extended to

Editorial Consultants

Alex Poinsett
Jerrie Cobb Scott
Gwendolyn Trotter
B. Denise Hawkins

and Editorial Assistants

Judy Beck
Tracy Leal Cecil
Cynthia J. Graddy
Barbara J. Olexer

A publication sponsored
by the

Charles Stewart Mott
Foundation

TABLE OF CONTENTS

PART I - RECONSTRUCTING OUR IDENTITY

FOREWORD

Unless you know the road you've come down, you cannot know where you are going.
–Tenne Proverb, Sierra Leone

David G. Imig
Arthur E. Wise

The student population in the United States is becoming more diverse. The teacher workforce, in contrast, is becoming less diverse, and it is likely to become even more white, suburban, and female because of the pending retirement of many of the teachers of color who have played such a prominent role in our schools. There is widespread recognition of the pressing need for more teachers of color. For a host of reasons, we need a socially and ethnically diverse teaching workforce. But we have been stymied in our ability to recruit, prepare, and place more candidates of color in teaching.

A primary source of teachers of color has been Historically Black Colleges and Universities (HBCUs). Many of the HBCUs were founded as teacher training institutes or normal schools, and they have long provided teachers to our local communities. Despite being constrained in their conduct of programs by many factors – including the impoverishment of resources and severe financial constraints – they have held on as a resource for African-American communities throughout the country.

Over time, though, the constraints imposed on HBCUs have diminished their ability to meet the expectations for teachers capable of teaching more challenging student populations in powerful ways. Within the structure of policies and practices imposed upon them by the state and others, they were forced to downsize programs and limit their outreach. In recognition of both the potential of the HBCUs to "scale up" and their historic role in producing significant numbers of African-American teachers, the National Council for Accreditation of Teacher Education (NCATE) and the American Association of Colleges for Teacher Education (AACTE) invested in a program to help the HBCUs refocus their efforts and expand their capabilities. Using the goal of professional, specialized accreditation as a vehicle to make fundamental changes in all aspects of HBCUs' teacher education programs, these organizations attracted grant funding and invested a talented, dedicated, and committed group of consultants in this endeavor.

This group of consultants joined with NCATE and AACTE professional staff to design a collaborative program of consultation, the HBCU Technical Support Network, that relies on extensive interactions between host institution and consultant. It is collaborative in that a special relationship is forged between HBCUs, the Association, and consultants. It is accountable in that the measure of success is the attainment of NCATE accreditation. The program derives strength from the Network – the other HBCUs and the consultants – who meet together, share successes and disappointments, and set new directions for the group. Indeed, one of the strongest features of this initiative is the sense of collegiality within the group and the forging of a professional community.

This book presents a set of cases that illustrates the vital work of this initiative. They tell the story of how HBCUs transformed themselves and fashioned stronger programs capable of producing more and better African-American teachers. It is a success story that deserves both wider recognition and the active and ongoing support of the philanthropic community.

We are indebted to Donna Gollnick, Cynthia J. Graddy, Barbara J. Olexer, Carol E. Smith, and Boyce C. Williams for their leadership of this initiative. We are particularly appreciative of the leadership of the core group of consultants. They have been superb in their efforts to make the HBCU initiative a viable, recognized, and rewarding priority for both AACTE and NCATE.

David G. Imig,   Arthur E. Wise,
President   President
AACTE   NCATE

PREFACE

If you don't tell your story, it'll get told and you won't even recognize it.

Sharon Robinson, Senior Vice President and Educational Testing Service Chief Operating Officer AACTE Annual Meeting, Chicago, Illinois, 1996

This eloquent remark given to the Technical Support Network Consultants sparked the idea for a volume telling the story of Historically Black institutions and their quest for quality teacher education through national accreditation. Because of this inspiration, it was only fitting that *Reforming Teacher Education Through Accrediatation: Telling Our Story* would be the volume's title.

Reform reports, professional groups, policymakers and the public are calling for higher standards for teacher prepration. Requirements for teacher preparation and performance are in the midst of great change. Bringing coherence to these efforts is the first challenge for the 21st century. AACTE and NCATE are poised to accept this challenge.

AACTE is a national, voluntary association of colleges and universities with undergraduate or graduate programs to prepare professional educators. It has and continues to play a major role in teacher education reform. The 736 AACTE member institutions graduate approximately 90 percent of the nation's new teachers and other educators each year.

NCATE too, is a voluntary organization, and has played a major role in upgrading teacher preparation standards. The United States Department of Education recognizes NCATE as the accrediting body for teacher preparation. NCATE's 506 accredited institutions and 70 candidates for accreditation produce approximately 70 percent of the nation's new teachers each year. Professional accreditation is a mark of distinction and a "stamp of approval" from the field at large which says that the institution has made a commitment to upgrade its teacher preparation programs and meet national professional standards.

Through the financial generosity of the Mott Foundation and the Eli Lilly Endowment, and the continuing substantive support of NCATE and AACTE, the HBCUTSN has grown into a successful technical assistance program that has reached far beyond the parameters of Historically Black Colleges and Universities into the national education community. The services, resources, and materials developed by the HBCUTSN continue to be in demand by all types of institutions.

This volume will highlight the history of HBCU's and the HBCUTSN, featuring case studies and reflections on how institutions have used NCATE accreditation to advance reform of their teacher education programs. It is intended to be informative for the teacher, insightful for the educator and beneficial for all students.

OVERVIEW

Value of Case Studies

Howard University

This case walks the reader through the whole accreditation process, from pre-conditions to rejoinders to the BOE report. It offers specific strategies for getting the job done, e.g., Quality Circles and Wednesday Happenings. The main theme is that challenges are met at "the Capstone," an insider's name for Howard University, with zeal, dignity, and success.

Xavier University of New Orleans

As a private Catholic institution, Xavier's story focuses less on the external mandates for NCATE accreditation and more on its internal mandate for using accreditation as a means of enriching its "pass-it-on tradition." Unlike the other cases, emphasis is placed on maintaining its identity as an institution dedicated to working toward a more just and humane world. The case emphasizes the importance of ongoing collegial reflection and dialogue on issues affecting the very existence of life and community survival in the coming millennium.

Delaware State University

As suggested by the title of this case study, Weaving Outcomes into the Fabric of the Program, Delaware State University's story relates some of the challenges to getting a good mix between program elements and the NCATE standards. Like none of the other cases, it presents viewpoints of an NCATE co-chair, revealing some of the questions that NCATE coordinators are likely to ask and pointing to some of the areas that NCATE coordinators should consider as they prepare to facilitate the process of preparing for accreditation. This case reminds the reader of the importance of entering the process with foresight, rather than blindly entering and becoming dependent on hindsight as the driving force for actions.

LeMoyne-Owen College

As a follow-up to the Delaware story, the LeMoyne-Owen case places the challenges to administrators at the center of its move toward stability. It is the only case that includes the perspective of the president of the institution. It reinforces the idea that collaborating for stability requires support from the bottom-up as well as the top-down. Uniquely, it also provides a mechanism, i.e., collaborating with non-HBCUs, that might be considered by predominantly African-American and predominantly White institutions for addressing the diversity standards.

Virginia Union University

This case presents the quest for accreditation as a "family affair." It shows how a major disaster, a fire, served as the catalyst for pulling people together. Prior to this disaster, the strivings for NCATE accreditation might have been perceived as a trip to a land of validation. After the disaster, the trip became more like a journey. More than any other case, this one embraces the notion that NCATE accreditation is not a trip but a step toward a journey of many miles, a journey that can actually lead to an ongoing process of improvement and growth.

General

The introduction provides the context for the evolution of HBCUs, and each case provides a glimpse of the institution's historical development. The reader will likely appreciate seeing the similarities and differences in the historical development of these institutions. The cases in this book show parallels, a positive development given the fact that each represents interventions from the HBCU network. This means that most talk about the various stages of the network's model: assessing, educating, coaching, and collaborating. Like the network itself, collaborating is one of the key themes at the heart of all other phases; therefore, collaboration is a recurring motif throughout the cases.

The reader will find that each institution developed strategies that provide springboards for others to think about how to approach the processes of preparing for accreditation and managing growth and improvement. There are enough situations here to provide a link to many of the typical problems that HBCUs face, creating comfort zones for those who may see their individual situation as having uniquely difficult barriers that seem impossible to hurdle. Here the space for complaining shrinks as the institutions fill their spaces with productive work. In the end, such work can result in a win-win situation for the people, including faculty, students, staff, and administrators, as well as for the programs, including the various re-forming and re-packaging initiatives that some of us refer to as significant progress toward systemic reform in the education of teachers.

ACKNOWLEDGEMENTS

Many people have played critical roles in developing this case study book. A special thank you is extended to Arthur E. Wise, President of the National Council for Accreditation of Teacher Education, whose vision and unselfish leadership created the context in which this project came to fruition as a part of his goal to ensure that every child in America is taught by a qualified teacher.

Acknowledgement and appreciation are extended to Donna Rhodes. Without her belief in it, her encouragement, and her undying support, this book would not have been possible.

The president of the institutions whose teacher education stories are told in this book deserve appreciation for their cooperation and forbearance as their educational units were dissected then resassembled. Trusting that they share the conviction that the result has been increased vigor, efficiency, and effectiveness, thanks go to William B. DeLauder, President, Delaware State University; H. Patrick Swygert, President, Howard University; George R. Johnson, Jr., President, LeMoyne-Owen College; S. Dallas Simmons, Immediate Past President, Virginia Union University; and Norman C. Francis, President, Xavier University of Louisiana.

INTRODUCTION

Sharon P. Robinson

Case studies reported in this book are important stories about change and commitment. When NCATE started the Historically Black Colleges and Universities Technical Support Network, I was intrigued and inspired by the courage of the participating institutions. Typically, they are underfunded; many of their students require significant academic and financial support; and they often find their mission challenged as irrelevant or unaffordable. It would have been understandable for these institutions to excuse themselves from the challenge of rigorous national accreditation standards.

The participants in this initiative were aware of their unique opportunity to improve their teacher education programs through the HBCU Technical Support Network. They were equally aware of their professional responsibility to extend themselves as researchers by carefully documenting their journey into reform and organizational development. The success of the Network is validated by the success of these programs in achieving accreditation. That is an impressive accomplishment. The reflections on the process captured in these case studies provide an opportunity for others to learn from their experiences.

It has been my privilege to support many reform

plans in P-12 education and in teacher education. These efforts are characterized by intense work in a cycle of planning, experimentation, coalition-building, and evaluation. Always, it seems, there is more risk involved in doing something than in doing nothing. And most often this work is in addition to the more traditional responsibilities associated with student learning and teacher development. This is difficult work – not for the faint of heart.

Often the work gets done – new processes are invented, and student learning improves. But telling the story in an organized fashion is left for a more convenient time, so the story never gets told. Fortunately, that will not be the case in this instance. Part I provides the context for networking in HBCUs, from the past to the present with the HBCU Technical Support Network. At the heart of the book are the stories of work within the framework of the Technical Support Network. Part II, the final two chapters, sets forth lessons and guidelines for the unit structure—pathways for the professional community and the Network and opportunities for collaboration.

We will not have to speculate about the process and the benefits of accreditation for HBCUs. We do not have to theorize about this unique population of institutions. We can learn from the perspective of those who have had the actual experience the important nuances that give meaning to the particulars, as shown in this volume.

Part I

RECONSTRUCTING OUR IDENTITY

Never have so few been called upon to do so much.
–Winston Churchill

CHAPTER 1

CHALLENGES AND COLLABORATIONS IN HISTORICALLY BLACK COLLEGES AND UNIVERSITIES

Boyce C. Williams

Historically Black Colleges and Universities (HBCUs) have had to overcome many obstacles during the course of their existence. For decades, HBCUs have responded to these challenges by engaging in cooperative ventures with religious denominations and private philanthropists. These alliances have allowed HBCUs to advocate for and find ways to educate large numbers of African-Americans for over a century.

As we move into the next century, HBCUs face one of their greatest challenges yet—preserving and renewing their mission of educating teachers. Teacher preparation has been a major focus of HBCUs since 1865, when the creation of the Freedmen's Bureau spurred the development of elementary schools for African-Americans and a corresponding need for more teachers. Enriching this tradition remains a priority at these institutions.

From the past to the present, collaborative efforts have facilitated the preparation of African-American teachers. This chapter presents a context for the stories told in this volume by providing an overview of these efforts, including an introduction of the creation of one of the most recent collaborations to improve teacher preparation in HBCUs—the HBCU Teacher Education Technical Support Network.

Past Challenges and Collaboratives in HBCUs

Perhaps no ideological framework had a greater impact on African-Americans' quest for higher education than democratization. That concept was discussed quite explicitly in the mid-19th century as a goal for higher education, and it accounted in part for the admission of African-Americans to colleges. While historical accounts of early African-American graduates are not precise, it has been documented that during the 1820s, three were awarded degrees from U.S. colleges: John Brown Russwurm from Bowdoin College in Maine, Edward Jones from Amherst College in Massachusetts, and Alexander Twilight from Middlebury College in Vermont (Kujovich, 1993). By the 1830s, Oberlin College in Ohio and Berea College in Kentucky had given special attention to providing higher education opportunities for African-Americans. By the turn of the century, however, Kentucky had outlawed racial integration in all public and private colleges. Meanwhile, three Black colleges were established: Cheyney and Lincoln in Pennsylvania and Wilberforce in Ohio. In the latter half of the 19th century and the early part of the 20th century, nearly 100 additional Black colleges were founded, mostly in the Southern states. As Kujovich points out:

> For many years private Black institutions produced the majority of Black college graduates, but the incessant demand of the Black population for education and the need for teachers to satisfy that demand led some state legislatures to fund Black normal

schools shortly after the Civil War. In the context of a general hostility toward and fear of Black education, state support for the training of Black teachers was usually given, if at all, only as an unpleasant alternative to the intrusion of Northern White teachers of Black elementary schools. (p. 74)

Cooperative efforts of Black religious denominations and private philanthropy significantly influenced state and federal government acceptance of and commitment to sharing the burden of educating African-Americans. The land-grant colleges, or state agricultural and mechanical schools, supported largely by the federal government, were established under the Morrill Act of 1862, with land-grant colleges offering some courses in teacher training. In 1890, the Second Morrill Act was established to ensure a more equitable distribution of land-grant funds, which aided in the establishment of separate schools for Blacks with support from state and federal funds. Dilworth notes that less than ten years after the Second Morrill Act, "expenditures on White land-grant colleges exceeded those for Black colleges by a ratio of 26 to one" (1984: 14, *Teachers Totter*). It was through the cooperative efforts of the John F. Slater Fund and the public school authorities of certain Southern states that county training schools, essentially rural high schools, were organized and maintained. In turn, training schools supplemented the elementary school facilities of the county and prepared students to teach elementary grades in rural areas (1984: 15).

The dual system of education was upheld by the U.S. Supreme Court's 1896 *Plessy v. Ferguson* decision, which sanctioned "separate but equal" facilities, thus institutionalizing inequities that continue to the present. Kujovich (1993) argues that because most states provided little support for Black elementary schools and almost no support for Black high schools, the early and widespread neglect of the Black land-grant colleges produced institutions that could not provide adequate higher education.

Conditions in Black land-grant colleges before World War I were deplorable, largely because support from the federal government and various civic and church funding sources was meager. Many of the buildings were dilapidated and ramshackled, with few blackboards, laboratories, maps, and other equipment vital to teaching. The living conditions of students and teachers were unsanitary. Other inadequacies included teachers' pay, faculty training, and library holdings and facilities.

Then as now, the issues of competency testing and certification were controversial. Here again there is some evidence of collaborative efforts to improve teacher preparation. Citing the report of a Virginia school inspector, Dilworth (1984) shows that Black teacher training programs were not given the same opportunities as their White counterparts. The report of the school inspector is reminiscent of problems today:

Of the 854 teachers, 377 were admitted on diplomas from recognized institutions and 477 passed examinations by the state. The 477 who passed constituted only 36 percent of the total who took the examination. Only 28 received first grade certificates, 169 were second grade, and 280 were third grade. The appalling number of failures and the low grade of the majority of the certificates can mean but one thing—the inadequacy of the preparation of the applicants. This inadequacy of preparation is fundamental, reaching down into the elementary schools. How, then, with inadequate elementary schools, or at least schools taught by inadequately prepared teachers, can we hope to improve our class of teachers? A careful survey of the situation points to but two sources from which relief may be expected—a greater number of publicly supported agencies for teacher training and a closer cooperation between the public school authorities and the existing private secondary schools for Negroes. (1984:16)

Dilworth (1984) points to agencies that were involved in cooperative efforts to redress the problems: "The state supervisors of Negro schools, the organization of county training schools, the supervisors of rural schools, the Jeanes Fund industrial teachers, the Peabody Education Fund, and the U.S. Bureau of Education, all made steps to improve the education and teaching methods of Black students." (p.15) Kujovich summarizes conditions with respect to teaching:

A system of higher education with the primary function of training teachers for segregated schools had produced a professional class that was composed primarily of teachers—more than 60 percent of all Black professionals compared with only 26 percent for the White professional class. Indeed, if teachers and clergymen (frequently graduates of private Black colleges) are excluded, the Black share of remaining professionals drops to less than 4 percent, for a population that made up 20 percent of the workforce. (p. 82)

Dilworth (1984) chronicles the continuing conditions of the early to mid-1900s:

In 1911, the majority of elementary teachers had only high school diplomas. In 1930, only seven of the Southern Black colleges were given approval status by the Southern Association of Colleges and Schools, larger numbers became accredited in 1961. In 1935, the average salary for a teacher in a Black elementary school was $510 a year, compared with $833 for Whites. In 1941, not a single full-time Black classroom teacher taught in a Northern institution of higher education, although there were a sizable number of Blacks with Ph.D. degrees. (pp. 16-17)

Again, cooperative initiatives proved fruitful. For example, to address the inequitable pay, Black teachers formed alliances with teacher unions. With the formation of national accreditation systems in the 1940s and 1950s, Blacks formed alliances with each other to meet the standards. The teacher shortage problem was exacerbated by the reluctance of Southern Whites to teach in Black elementary schools. In the book *Ready from Within* (Brown 1990) Septima Clark (1990) recounts her experiences with White teachers who refused to speak to Black children outside of school or to provide caring instruction inside. Conversely, African-Americans generally were committed to more humane, respectful teaching of African-Americans.

Many Black teachers continue to face problems in such crucial areas as compensation, employment, and licensing. While demands for teacher competency and certification are not new, more stringent state laws threaten the supply of Black teachers and the future of teacher training programs at HBCUs. In short, many of the historical inequities imposed on the education of Black teachers still linger today. Dilworth notes:

> While Black educators continue to champion equality of education, they would do well to keep in mind the role of Black teachers' colleges as iterated by H. Council Trenholm in 1942 in the *Journal of Negro Education.* He advocated that the Negro college conceive of its distinctive function with clarity, wisdom, and vision; anticipate a marked modification in the content of its curriculum; provide for a markedly advanced degree of thoroughness in the work of its students; accept the obligation to apply more rigid, intelligently administered selective admission procedures; and give added preparation which the circumstances of the Negro participation in our national life makes most imperative. (1984:21)

The 1989 report of the Committee on Policy for Racial Justice, *Vision of a Better Way: A Black Appraisal of Public Schooling,* summarized lessons learned from the past:

One (lesson) is certainly that Black people have shown a persistent commitment to schooling, as demonstrated by their struggle and sacrifice. Even under the most trying circumstances Black communities have energetically organized their social resources and political will to improve the education of their children. Committed student-teacher relationships and the dedication of Black educators who strove against the odds created an infrastructure for Black intellectual advancement. Another lesson is that the concept of education for the Black community has implicitly adopted—education for liberation, for citizenship, for personal and collective power and advancement—has deep roots. (1989:11-12)

As HBCUs have evolved in recent decades, they have faced the need to link their historical tradition of building collaborative alliances with the implementation of systematic planning for the future. Like other higher education institutions, HBCUs have developed strategic plans that include long-term goals, usually five years, and short-term goals, annual targets or indicators for achieving incremental changes. Managing change means that units within an institution both support institutional goals and develop additional goals to meet specific needs of units.

The HBCU Technical Assistance Model and Process

In 1995, the Lilly Endowment, Inc., provided funding to the National Council for Accreditation of Teacher Education for a project to help HBCUs strengthen their preparatory programs for P-12 teachers. Consequently, the HBCU Teacher Education Technical Support Network was created to support HBCUs in their efforts to strengthen their programs and to become nationally accredited. The Network enabled institutions to more fully and consciously utilize their past experiences with collaboratives and with the accreditation process to improve the overall quality of teacher education programs. Each of the cases describes critical moments in the institution's work with the Network. This discussion of the Technical Assistance Model is intended to provide a basic point of reference for the institutions' discussions of their move through various stages of the model. The accreditation route is one way for HBCUs to preserve and renew their tradition of educating teachers, a process that would be facilitated by the HBCU Technical Assistance Model and Process. When the project began in 1995, there were 101 four-year Historically and Traditionally Black Colleges and Universities. Of the 101, 82 (81%) offered four-year degrees in education. By the end of 1999,

- 58 (71%) were members of AACTE;
- 50 (61%) were accredited by NCATE;
- 5 (6.0%) were candidates for NCATE accreditation;
- 6 (7%) were pre-candidates for NCATE accreditation.

Thus, of the 82 HBCUs that prepare teachers, 61 (74%) were members of the NCATE family as accredited institutions, candidates, or pre-candidates, up from 39 (48%) when the project began only two years earlier. Two factors underscored the strategic importance of the Technical Assistance project: 1) HBCUs train over 50 percent of all African-American students, and 2) expanding opportunities in other fields have paralleled increases in the total number of college-trained African-Americans, but these trends have not increased the number entering the teaching profession. Hence HBCUs are challenged to produce more and better-prepared teachers.

In forming this collaborative network of support, initial conversations among the American Association of Colleges for Teacher Education, NCATE, and a number of HBCU presidents identified potential concerns, directions, and benefits as well as the potential impact of the project on HBCU teacher preparation programs. From these dialogues emerged a four-phase model for assisting HBCUs. A second grant, this one from the Charles Stewart Mott Foundation, enabled the project to fully implement the model and provide a broad range of Network services to institutions selected jointly by NCATE and AACTE.

Key aspects of the model are consultants experienced both with HBCUs and with the nuts and bolts of technical assistance, the networking model that they, along with staff created, and the processes in which they were engaged.

Consultants

Network consultants were selected because of their expertise and commitment to the important role of HBCUs in training P-12 teachers. During a two-day training seminar, the consultants learned the competencies, expectations, and responsibilities that they should demonstrate in their relations with HBCUs.

Consultant training was supported by an extensive manual developed by lead consultants and project staff. The manual is intended for use in the training process and as an on-site tool during campus visits. Among other resources, the manual provides templates to guide specific parts of the consulting and reporting processes. Network teams range from two to five members. One team member serves as chair or team leader and is responsible for the overall conduct of the campus visit. To avoid conflict of interest and questionable or improper activities, consultants follow professional and ethical principles that guide relationships between institutions and consultants.

Network consultants were assigned to work with institutions on the basis of their experience and expertise related to teacher education, accreditation, and program development. They did not officially represent either AACTE or NCATE, but rather, relied on professional judgment to prepare needs assessment reports and advise institutions about the best ways to present evidence of high-quality programs. These reports do not reflect official NCATE evaluations, because such judgments are made when the Board of Examiners (BOE) team assigned by NCATE conducts its on-site review and reports to the board that renders the final accreditation decision, the Unit Accreditation Board. Hence, the Network was careful to specify that consultant advice should not be regarded as a "guarantee" that the professional education unit will achieve accreditation at its initial review.

These specially trained consultants became the nucleus of the Network. The consultants conducted needs assessments and mock accreditation visits at HBCUs to help faculty and staff at those institutions in their efforts to improve the quality of their teacher education programs.

The consultants addressed a wide range of issues such as 1) sensitivity to circumstances unique to the institution or its education unit; 2) confidentiality and access to institutional data; 3) effective procedures for conducting the needs assessment required as an initial step in the accreditation process; 4) understanding of the Network model; and 5) appropriate interactions with various campus constituencies.

The Network Model

"HBCUs must demonstrate quality in everything they do; thus teacher preparation programs must produce quality graduates," Kentucky State University Immediate Past President Mary L. Smith told the consultants at their first training session. She cited rigorous accreditation standards as keys to excellence in teacher preparation. Network success in this endeavor ensures improvements in the production of P-12 teachers who can effectively educate an increasingly diverse student population. The Network incorporates four phases in its technical assistance model—assessing, educating, coaching, and collaborating. These four phases are dynamic components of an ongoing institutional process.

FACILITATION PROCESS FOR TECHNICAL SUPPORT

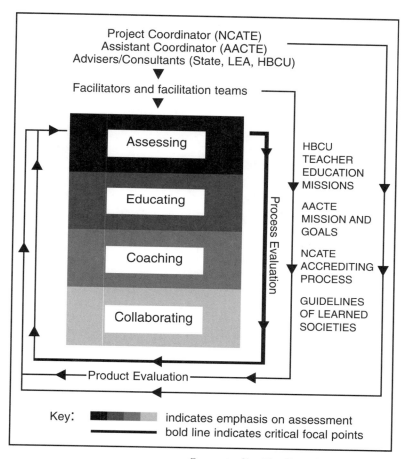

Project Coordinator (NCATE)
Assistant Coordinator (AACTE)
Advisers/Consultants (State, LEA, HBCU)

Facilitators and facilitation teams

Assessing

Educating

Coaching

Collaborating

Process Evaluation

HBCU TEACHER EDUCATION MISSIONS

AACTE MISSION AND GOALS

NCATE ACCREDITING PROCESS

GUIDELINES OF LEARNED SOCIETIES

Product Evaluation

Key: ▬▬▬ indicates emphasis on assessment
——— bold line indicates critical focal points

Conceptualized by Gwendolyn Trotter

This model represents an operational view of the HBCUTSN. The strategies used throughout the Network process are based on institutional mission, accreditation policy and procedure guidelines of participating professional associations, and professional development practices. The conceptualization for this model came through the work of Gwendolyn Trotter during her professorial experiences at Grambling State University, Grambling, Louisiana. Coordination of the project is under the direction of NCATE and AACTE. Facilitators and facilitation teams are representatives of HBCUs and state education and local education agencies that have demonstrated excellent skills and leadership in the accreditation and higher education process. The most important feature of the model is its emphasis on continual assessment.

HBCUTSN MODEL -- STAGES AND ACTIVITIES*

ASSESSING	EDUCATING	COACHING	COLLABORATING
• Needs Assessment Visit	• Development/ Implementation of Unit Improvement Activities	• Professional Clinics	• Identification of Technical Assistance Ability/Needs
• Needs Assessment Instrument	• Development/ Implementation of Faculty Activities	• Continued Faculty Professional Development Activities	• Establishment of Professional Development Networks
• Institutional Analysis	• Additional Visits by Lead Consultant and Continued Written and Oral Communication	• Simulated Accreditation Visits	• Sharing of Resources and Experiences
• Consultant Cadre Analysis			
• Faculty Interviews			
• Unit Documentation			
• NCATE Standards			
• Needs Assessment Report			

* The original Network Model, Facilitation Process for Technical Support Network, can be found in the Appendices

Assessing. The first phase of consulting with institutions is conducting a needs assessment. This process builds systems for change in teacher preparation and develops consensus on curriculum and programs. Guided by NCATE standards, consultants and institution representatives identify program elements that should be strengthened for NCATE review. The assessment also develops faculty consensus on the purpose and direction of any needed changes. The needs assessment process initiates conversations between faculty in the institution and consultants, who bring not only expertise but also additional perspectives and connections with off-campus professional groups.

Educating. The second consulting phase, educating, involves curriculum design and delivery and faculty development. Consultants work with institutions to address weaknesses in these areas identified by the needs assessment.

Coaching. The third consulting phase, coaching, documents changes and activities and enables consultants to evaluate the prior two phases. In helping institutions document and review their activities, consultants set the stage for the self-study by the institution that is required by the accreditation process. During this phase, institutions receive simulated accreditation visits.

Collaborating. In the fourth and final phase, collaborating, institutions share resources with on-campus colleagues and with other institutions that are preparing for accreditation reviews. This stage enhances the capacity of institutions to 1) identify resources they may need from other sources in the education community; 2) establish a professional development network to promote self-generated improvement of teacher education programs; and 3) serve as resources for other institutions undergoing accreditation reviews or program changes.

Several key factors characterize the model and are essential to its successful use at any institution. One is the use of trained consultants, particularly in the early phases of the model. Network consultants are trained extensively in various approaches to consulting in higher education institutions as well as in the knowledge and skills related to NCATE's accreditation process. Another key factor of the model is its emphasis on review by Network consultants outside the institution.

A final key to successful use of the Network model is faculty consensus during every stage of the process. Indeed, a primary function of the needs assessment process is to promote conversation and self-reflection among the faculty responsible for the design and delivery of teacher education. As the institution proceeds through the subsequent phases of educating, coaching, and collaborating, active engagement of the faculty is essential to developing a smooth, ongoing cycle of assessment and improvement.

The Process

In spring 1995, institutions eligible to join the project were required to analyze their readiness for the accreditation process and determine whether they could meet the challenges presented by a national accreditation review. They applied for participation in the project knowing that the institutions selected must commit time, resources, faculty, and staff. A review committee of representatives from Network consultants, the higher education community, and project staff evaluated the applications. Acceptance into the Network was based on institutional commitment, preparation for accreditation review, anticipated need, and institutional mission. Letters of agreement that outlined the project goals, policies, and procedures, as well as the institution's role and responsibilities, were sent to 11 selected institutions in June 1995.

Consultants were matched with institutions and organized in teams of three to five members. A lead consultant was designated to chair the needs assessment visit and oversee communication with the institution and project staff.

Schedules were set for the needs assessment visits. Visits followed a three-day schedule, using templates developed by project staff and lead consultants. Each needs assessment visit included discussion between consultants and staff on a common instrument that incorporated major themes of the NCATE standards. Consultant teams reviewed a variety of evidence related to these themes. Types of evidence presented varied by institution. As an exercise in advance of the visit, faculty rated their own success on each dimension; after reviewing the relevant evidence, consultants conferred with key members of the unit's faculty and central administration to present the consultants' rating. They discussed any variations in the two evaluations of the unit's success in addressing themes and talked about the kinds of evidence the consultants had reviewed. Each needs assessment review was summarized in a written report that consultants provided to the institution shortly after the visit.

The needs assessment process served as a foundation for the consulting process. It set the stage for an interactive relationship between faculty and administrators from the campus on one side, and the consultant team and project staff on the other. The self-assessment completed by faculty established early ownership of the process by the full professional education unit, not just the small leadership group. In addition, the format and instruments of the needs assessment focused the process on evidence, ensuring that discussions and decisions were based on factual information. Finally, the needs assessment process was crucial as the first step in establishing a consensus on the institution's agenda for teacher education—"What are the strengths we can build on? Where do we need to focus our attention and energy?"

This opening process set the stage for the second phase of the network model: educating. It began with conversations between consultants and faculty on how to transform results of the needs analysis into priorities and activities that would prepare the unit for NCATE review and address important unit goals. An essential element in the educating phase was identifying areas in which faculty needed to construct their own research agendas or professional development in order to address weaknesses highlighted by the needs assessment process. Again, the collaborative work with consultants enabled faculty to develop on-campus professional clinics and to identify opportunities at regional and national conferences that would address professional development needs. An interesting aspect that emerged during the educative phase was early identification of strategies for addressing needed changes in the program. This was particularly true as faculty built networks with colleagues from around the country.

Transition to an emphasis on coaching began to happen as faculty actually carried out the program improvement efforts formulated in the early stages of the HBCU Technical Support Network's work.

This phase of the project marked a point at which consultants began to take more of a back-seat role as coaches so that faculty and administrators could take full ownership of the changes and evidence-building process. At this point, faculty were likely to come to consultants with more targeted questions and requests for advice. The culmination of this phase was usually a mock visit—typically by a combination of Network consultants and others knowledgeable about the accreditation process. Again, as with the needs assessment, the institution received a full report from the team, detailing strengths, weaknesses, and areas where evidence was not available.

Institutions participating in the Network project often moved into the final phase—collaborating—without actually recognizing the shift. They began making presentations on their work, discussing accreditation and teacher education improvement with colleagues, and reaching out in numerous directions. Some faculty expressed interest in training for Board of Examiners service. All institutions increased their attendance at and participation in national conferences. The Network institutions began working with each other to compile case studies for this book.

The framework for the Network consulting model proved to be an effective one. It provided for early identification of goals to guide the project in each institution, continuing opportunities to reassess progress and gain access to new resources, and sources of support for moving through the inevitable ups and downs as faculty struggled to make program changes and strengthen documentation. The process did not operate in exactly the same manner at each institution. Some spent longer in particular phases, and some found they needed to bring in multiple sets of consultants in order to facilitate a wider range of activities. The common denominators for all were self-assessment combined with external review and the building of a community to accomplish this work. In the cases that follow, institutions describe their experiences. The reader will find common strands across the institutions, different strategies for attaining results, and unique circumstances, all converging to show how these institutions used the goal of professional, specialized accreditation as a vehicle to make fundamental changes in different aspects of their teacher education programs.

Acknowledgements

Special thanks are extended to Mary E. Dilworth, senior research director at the American Association of Colleges for Teacher Education. Her writing and research featured in the below referenced report helped to develop the framework and fine-tune this chapter.

References

Brown, Cynthia Stokes (ed.). (1986) *Ready from Within: Septima Clark and the Civil Rights Movement (A First Person Narrative)*. Navarro, CA: Wild Trees Press

The Committee on Policy for Racial Justice. (1989) *Visions of a better way: A black appraisal of public schooling*. Washington, D.C.: Joint Center for Political Studies Press

Dilworth, Mary E. (1984) *Teachers' Totter: A report on teacher certification issues.* Washington, D.C.: Institute for the Study of Educational Policy, Howard University

Kujovich, Gil. (1993/94, Winter) "Public Black colleges: The long history of unequal funding." *The Journal of Blacks in Higher Education* 2, 73-82

Chapter 2

Challenges At The Capstone Howard University

Mary B. Conley
Veronica G. Thomas

The leadership of Howard University (HU) in Washington, D.C., has always envisioned an institution that provides quality education of the highest order for its students. At a meeting of some of the university's founding fathers in 1866, it was proposed that this new institution for Blacks (coloreds) be called The Howard Normal and Theological Institute for the Education of Teachers and Preachers. The preparation of teachers and practitioners has been a part of the fabric of the institution from its beginning. On January 8, 1867, the trustees of the institute agreed that its name would be Howard University (Logan, 1969). The Howard University Charter, a bill enacted by Congress on March 2, 1867, provided for the education of youth in the liberal arts and sciences (Logan, 1969). The word "youth" in the bill included education not only for Blacks but also for women. From its inception, HU—"the Mecca," "the Capstone," as it is fondly referred to by its students, alumnae and alumni, faculty, and community members—has valued diversity as it focused on excellence in the preparation of its students.

HU is the world's largest and most comprehensive historically Black university. It is one of only 88 universities in the country designated a level-one research university by the Carnegie Foundation for the Advancement of Teaching. HU is a coeducational, private institution with more than 2,000 faculty members and 11,000 students from more than 90 countries. It is one of 101 historically and predominantly Black four-year colleges and universities in the United States, and one of the 82 that offers four-year degrees in education. The School of Education, one of the university's 16 colleges and schools, was elevated to the level of a separate school in 1971. It offers programs resulting in bachelor's, master's, and doctoral degrees. The School of Education has as its mission the preparation of students who will become *"Educators and Practitioners who are Facilitators of Change, Reflective Professionals, and Scholarly Researchers,"* and who will assume *leadership roles in the global society.*

In keeping with the university's historical legacy, Dr. H. Patrick Swygert, the 15th president of HU, communicated a need for the university to build on its foundation of excellence while making itself relevant for the 21st century. President Swygert presented his "Strategic Framework for Action" to the university community in early 1996. The focal point of the plan was the strengthening of academic programs and services. Since he became president in 1995, President Swygert has made clear that accredited programs are essential if the university is to measure up to its legacy of excellence.

Thus, the School of Education's effort to seek national accreditation was consistent with the president's "Strategic Framework for Action." Although the school had begun preparing for accreditation more than a year earlier, the "Strategic Framework for Action" provided the school's administration with much-needed leverage for the seemingly difficult task that lay ahead—a quest for national accreditation from the National Council for Accreditation of Teacher Education. This accreditation "work in progress" would ultimately receive outstanding support and services from the Historically Black Colleges and Universities Technical Support Network.

The School of Education planned a joint NCATE/state visit, a collaborative effort conducted by NCATE's Board of Examiners (BOE) and the District of Columbia's review team to assess the quality of the School of Education and its 15 programs. Unfortunately, the process was hampered by changes in assignment among faculty, staff, and administrators. Nonetheless, it was vital that we quickly adjust to these changes and continue on. Given that the School of Education was on this important quest for accreditation, we could not turn back—we were determined to keep our eyes on the prize—receiving NCATE accreditation in spring 1997. This report chronicles the process and activities related to the NCATE portion of the visit.

Challenge I: The Ultimate Analysis—Looking at Ourselves

As the School of Education prepared for NCATE, there was a rekindled sense of energy and an air of excitement among the faculty. Although the school first perceived a quest for national accreditation as a daunting task, we accepted the challenge. The faculty viewed accreditation as an opportunity to improve our teacher education program, to turn excellent teaching into outstanding instruction, and to integrate traditional instructional materials with instructional technology required to ensure student success in the 21st century. The HBCU Technical Support Network provided the means for the critical analysis the school needed to be successful in our quest.

One of the most difficult aspects of the process was getting started. This meant initially addressing the 10 conditions and preparing the preconditions report required by NCATE (NCATE, 1995). Satisfying this requirement signaled the School of Education's readiness for pursuing NCATE accreditation. If an institution or unit were unable to address these qualifying milestones, interest in proceeding would surely wane. While we were aware of the theoretical need to involve the entire faculty, meeting deadlines gave way to expeditiousness. As we prepared responses for the preconditions report in winter 1995, some of the faculty members were only marginally involved. We were delighted by the spirit of cooperation demonstrated by some faculty members and chairs who worked days, evenings, and even weekends to get the job done.

We found out later, however, the importance of involving the *entire* faculty in the process—not just selected faculty, staff, and administrators. Empowering the faculty to address a variety of issues and concerns was very important in the analysis of our programs and processes. Finding ways to include and engage all faculty and staff was critical to successful accreditation work and ultimately to the attainment of excellence in our teacher education and practitioner programs.

Next, we were concerned about the needs assessment visit, as described in the HBCU Network's Consultant's Manual (NCATE, 1995), which was conducted by a Network team of consultants in April 1995. Initially, we were nervous. Our dean stated that the Network team "was positive, supportive, yet frank and honest in relating our program's strengths and weaknesses to the indicators in the needs assessment instrument." Like many groups and individuals, we gave ourselves a higher ranking in several categories than did members of the assessment team.

After the team left, we held our collective breath until we received the assessment report. There were few surprises. However, when we reviewed the results, we knew that we had some work to do if we were going to address successfully the 20 standards and 69 indicators in the *NCATE Standards, Procedures, and Policies for the Accreditation of Professional Education Units* (NCATE, 1995). The School of Education found out in May 1995 that HU was eligible for a Network grant to help us through the process. This meant that we would receive the services of well-prepared and highly qualified consultants from the Network. We would soon find this service to be invaluable. The team consultants could provide us with direct consulting services or professional clinics. As requested, the Network also would recommend other individuals or services to address specific needs identified by the School of Education.

At this point, excitement escalated. The Network team's response to our needs assessment report and instrument provided direction for the School of Education's accreditation work and leveraged the school's priorities with the university's central administration. We realized after analyzing the report that if we were going to reach the pinnacle toward which this national accreditation work directs institutions—achieving excellence in their initial and advanced programs—*we could leave no stone unturned.*

Collectively, we would have to reexamine painstakingly our human resources, and we would have to review all of our programs, documents, and processes related to the teacher education and practitioner programs. We also needed to review the relationship with our partners, to determine their relevance to the NCATE standards, and we had to review the currency of their programs. This analysis meant that we might have to discard some vested interests or products that we had become attached to and align them with professional standards. The grant also funded professional clinics for faculty, staff, and external partners to work with experts who were experienced with and knowledgeable about the critical elements required for a successful quest for accreditation.

One of the first professional clinics we hosted was conducted by Dr. Gary Galluzzo during the School of Education's opening faculty retreat in summer 1995. Working with the entire faculty, the accreditation task group, the principal, and selected faculty from our Professional Development School, he provided a clearer understanding of a conceptual framework and its interactive sessions that used the concepts of cooperative learning. The activities that Dr. Galluzzo conducted enabled the group to define the conceptual framework and student outcomes and understand why they were central to programs in the School of Education. One of the most important aspects of the clinic was that all participants be involved in development and buy in to the concepts that enabled us to crystallize earlier work. We were now ready, as a unit, to synthesize and unify principles and beliefs embedded in the conceptual framework across all three departments in the School of Education (the Department of Curriculum and Instruction, the Department of Education Administration and Policy, and the Department of Human Development and Psycho-Educational Studies).

As the NCATE coordinator stated, "A well-defined and agreed-upon conceptual framework is critical to whatever we undertake. Its development should precede the review and revision of course syllabi, programs, school-wide and department brochures/materials, and pertinent evaluation materials." As a result of the professional clinic, the school formed a conceptual framework committee composed of representatives and volunteers from each of its three departments and the dean's office. The work of this committee, in conjunction with the faculty, was invaluable to the process. Focus groups, consisting of students, college faculty, school system faculty/staff, cooperating teachers, university administrators, members of the Teacher Education Advisory Council, and community partners were held to get input for the conceptual framework. After final review by the focus groups and the School of Education faculty, the conceptual framework was adopted in winter 1995.

Participation and invaluable contributions by members of the focus groups laid the groundwork for the School of Education to identify an appropriate conduit that would draw a variety of individuals into our working session. Including their diverse perspectives and interests related to teacher education was necessary if the School of Education was to meet *the Ultimate Challenge of Looking at Ourselves Critically*.

Henceforth, regularly scheduled meetings, which we eventually referred to as "NCATE Wednesday Happenings" began. We started each session with a planned agenda, but issues and concerns from attendees were welcomed. These meetings were held throughout the year, from the spring to the fall of 1996. Thus, we had continuity and time to complete products without interruptions from school vacations.

We were able to accomplish a mammoth task that required the review and subsequent revision of programs, processes, and documents within a department, across departments, and between schools and colleges. This analysis required great strength and courage on the part of many professionals within the university. The ultimate aim was to put aside personal needs in order to achieve the greater good. The "NCATE Wednesday Happenings" were invaluable to this cross-fertilization and to open communications. The quest for accreditation would eventually result in a greater cohesiveness and allegiance among the faculty toward a common good.

Working together toward the achievement of the mission, goals, and objectives of the School of Education and the university, the faculty would unify around the basic principles and beliefs of our conceptual framework—*preparing Educators and Practitioners who are Facilitators of Change,*

Reflective Professionals, and Scholarly Researchers and who will assume leadership roles in the global society. These students also would be able to provide "The Leadership for America" in keeping with the theme of the university.

Challenge II: The Preparation—Leave No Stone Unturned

In anticipation of results from the needs assessment visit, we decided to prepare ourselves as team members with much information and knowledge related to NCATE standards. While responses to the 25 indicators for the needs assessment instrument were based on a sample of information gleaned from the 20 NCATE standards, we knew that we had to familiarize ourselves with each of NCATE's 20 standards and 69 indicators. Two faculty members from the School of Education attended the orientation for institutions seeking initial accreditation in the summer of 1995. From that meeting, important lessons were learned that armed the School of Education with tools and strategies necessary to engage the task before us. We made contacts with several persons at the meeting who would subsequently provide professional clinics for the faculty. These professional clinics were conducted on the following topics: 1) developing the conceptual framework; 2) marketing the conceptual framework with appropriate materials and resources; and 3) setting up the documents room and cataloging the exhibits efficiently.

We now realized the relevance of the *seven strands* embedded in the NCATE standards to the design of quality teacher education programs at

HU. In the fall 1994 issue of *NCATE Quality Teaching*, the seven major themes that are integrated throughout the standards were described: High Quality, Collaboration, Diversity, Intellectual Vitality, Performance Expectations, Program Evaluation, and Technology. This reiteration of the seven themes reinforced the need for us to thoroughly understand their meaning and their application in our programs.

After we received the needs assessment report in May 1995, we realized that the school needed a comprehensive planning process—one that covered all of the recommendations in the HBCU Network needs assessment report and also provided for tasks related to the 20 standards. The plan included additional tasks related to the accreditation project, and others unfolded as we proceeded on our quest. The first important task was to send the report to the faculty and other relevant stakeholders. A "quality circle" was identified to develop tasks necessary for implementing recommendations from the needs assessment. This initial plan was for the period of August 16, 1995, to November 20, 1996. We later realized that this was only the beginning of writing and modifying plans for the accreditation process.

It was one thing for the accreditation team members to write the plan, but another to involve specific persons who had responsibility for resolving issues involved in meeting the standards. At first we did not make a concerted effort to identify the key implementers in the development of the plan but rather requested participation of the department chairs and faculty volunteers. We soon learned that key persons with needed information were not included in the quality circle. We lost precious time. Subsequently, we made personal contacts with faculty members who had critical information about the teacher education programs and who needed to be at the table when accreditation strategies were developed. We modified the method for identifying participants for the quality circles. We then began to move forward at a steady pace.

In May 1995, the plan focused on those issues identified in the needs assessment, but modification of the plan also became a routine part of our work cycle. As we forged new ground, we returned to the plan to include any new tasks. One of the early tasks required the development of a written conceptual framework that was grounded in theory and current research. A subtask was to make connections between the conceptual framework and the course syllabi, student outcomes, curriculum outcomes, and course objectives/course descriptors. Developing the conceptual framework proved to be the most difficult one to get all faculty involved in.

Faculty involvement was critical to achieving this task. Faculty members had to determine how the conceptual framework linked to their course syllabi, curriculum outcomes, and so forth. A standard format that contained the critical elements related to the conceptual framework and NCATE standards was developed. The format was discussed and approved in the May 1996 faculty meeting. Subsequently, the course outline was disseminated to each faculty member to ensure uniformity in addressing the pertinent standards. Because of the varied and personal work styles of individuals, this critical task associated with Standard I.A of the *1995 Revised Edition of NCATE Standards* required constant monitoring.

Department chairpersons secured course syllabi for documentation related to Standard I.A. This task would probably never be 100 percent completed. Why? Changes in faculty assignments, as well as the need for behavior modification by some faculty members, could not be mandated. Rather, regular communication and opportunities for involving faculty in the reform process were necessary. Changes or revisions in course syllabi consistent with the conceptual framework were part of an ongoing effort. The conceptual framework had to be evaluated regularly. If significant changes in the conceptual framework and/or course content occurred, then course syllabi and other program documents would need to be modified. Faculty members did link the conceptual framework to their teaching/classroom products.

In this phase, many of the processes and procedures of the School of Education were reviewed. Some required modification or documentation. Others were passed on by word of mouth. The accreditation team experienced some of this firsthand as we reviewed what we did, why we did it, and how we did it. At several meetings between May and July 1996, faculty and staff from the School of Education and the College of Arts and Sciences met to review the admission process and criteria for accepting students into the Five-Year Elementary or Secondary Teacher Education Programs. This was a classic example of the disconnect between what we thought we were doing and actual practices. It was interesting to hear several participants describe the process. Some related information based on what they did; others communicated information from old documents; still others based their descriptions on experiences from the past.

The beauty of the accreditation process was that weaknesses related to process were repaired as participants responsible for any aspect of the admissions process met in quality circles. Ways to define and document the admissions process, criteria, and timelines, along with the steps to be followed by the students and the faculty, were agreed upon by all parties. The proposed process was then disseminated to the faculty for comments. Finally came the important step of committing the approved process and procedures to writing and including them in all pertinent student materials and faculty/staff advising manuals (School of Education, 1996).

This cycle of reviewing programs, processes, procedures, and materials occurred repeatedly in 1996. Identifying quality circles to address specific accreditation standards and issues was very useful. The school reviewed and subsequently revised major documents such as Department Handbooks, the Faculty Advising Manual, the Student Handbook, the Field Placement Handbooks, the Student Teacher Handbook, and the Cooperating Teacher Handbook.

The Network grant also enhanced our working relationship with our professional development school, the Katie C. Lewis (KCL) Elementary School, as we worked on the standard related to collaboration. We were better able to support some of our KCL collaboratives financially. For example, when principal Joyce Thompson requested our assistance for several staff development activities, faculty members made excellent presentations on the topics she identified. For example, faculty members conducted a workshop for parents on how they could assist their children at home with learning activities. The funding facilitated the purchase of materials for making learning packets. We conducted classes at KCL. The KCL faculty joined in some of our faculty meetings and we in theirs. Now KCL children expect HU students and faculty members to be around KCL observing, telling stories, tutoring, practice-teaching, and counseling. We also sponsored a 5K run/walk to benefit the KCL science program. These activities became part of the evidence used to address the standard focused on collaboration.

Technology was one of the seven major themes in the standards, but technology was lacking in the School of Education when the preparation process began in earnest during the 1994-95 school year. While faculty members had access to computers, only a small number had computers in their offices. The School of Education building was not wired to the HU Net. Thus, access to the Internet and e-mail services was not available to the faculty, students, or staff in the building. Although computers were available elsewhere on campus, the faculty wanted to have technology regularly available for instructional projects and for other technology integration efforts. The general computer lab and the Instructional Materials Center (IMC) in the school, if graded, would probably have received a rating of two on a five-point scale. A subsequent survey by staff from the university's Information System and Automated Services (ISAS) center confirmed our lack of readiness in the area of technology. The school needed additional equipment and human resource support to meet technology standards.

University administrators granted our requests to use restricted resources in our budget to address our technology needs. By the time of the April 1996 mock accreditation visit, each faculty member had a computer in her or his office, as well as access to the Internet and e-mail services and selected training on how to use the new services. Computer labs were updated with several new computers and other relevant technology. Approximately 90 percent of the students requested and received e-mail addresses. While technology issues were not completely resolved, the school had come a long way toward meeting the technology standard.

By the time the accreditation visit occurred in November 1996, the outstanding technology issues had been addressed. Combination television and VCRs were installed in each of the classrooms in the School of Education. New typewriters, scanners, software, and overhead projectors were provided for each of the three labs and each of the three departments. The name of the Instructional Materials Center (IMC) was changed to Educational Technology Center (ETC) to reflect the school's greater emphasis on technology. The dean provided resources to hire students as computer lab assistants to meet our students' needs in the lab. Hours of operation were extended until 8 p.m. We were very proud of these accomplishments.

As the School of Education was about to begin the fall 1996 session, the accreditation team realized that we were in the countdown mode. Anxiety prevailed. Three critical tasks on the accreditation plan remained to be completed: 1) marketing the conceptual framework, 2) finalizing the institutional report, and 3) organizing the "living documents room." The team regrouped and began to map strategies for meeting the timeline. Meanwhile, the accreditation visit was 90 days away.

The conceptual framework had been completed. Linkages had been made relative to the course syllabi, program descriptors, course objectives, and student outcomes. The faculty were relatively comfortable with discussing the conceptual framework. However, the team needed to disseminate the conceptual framework to all relevant stakeholders, consistent with NCATE Standard I.A. We had developed a logo and model for the conceptual framework that was transferred onto different items.

Once the conceptual framework marketing materials were completed, team members assumed responsibility for delivering the products to assigned individuals. The logo on the materials was quite effective in helping the School communicate the meaning of the conceptual framework to the wider community. Ideas about this method of marketing the conceptual framework were presented to the faculty at a professional clinic by one of the HBCU Network consultants. While we started out using materials for communicating the conceptual framework, we subsequently realized that they were also helpful in our recruitment efforts.

During the last week of August 1996, the Board of Examiners chairperson pre-visited our campus and reviewed the requirements for a successful accreditation visit with the dean, key administrators, and selected faculty members. The chairperson was very knowledgeable, professional, and well-prepared to work with university people anxiously awaiting the visit date. The highlight of the agenda for this one-day meeting included reviewing all of the events slated to take place from Saturday through Wednesday when the five-member team arrived in Washington. Logistical requirements for the visit, as described in the *1996 Edition of the NCATE Handbook for Conducting Continuing Accreditation Visits*, were discussed thoroughly.

Prior to the pre-planning meeting, we sent a draft copy of the institutional report to the BOE team chair. He reviewed our documents and had no major concerns with the report, but he did identify some areas that we might need to clarify for the benefit of reviewers. The BOE chairperson indicated that once the team finalized the institutional report, the NCATE coordinator needed to forward the documents in a timely manner to the BOE members. At this juncture we decided to conduct a final and thorough review of the institutional report. Quality circles were identified that were compatible with sections of the standards. Faculty members' areas of expertise were matched with the assigned sections of the standards. Consequently, 1) faculty members in one quality circle would give their final approval of responses assigned to the standards for finalization of the institutional report; and 2) members in the second quality circle collected, synthesized, and organized the documents related to each of the standards for placement in the document room. Using quality circle members for the final review in these two areas helped us complete the institutional report and exhibits required for the documents room.

Approximately three weeks before the visit, the team prepared accreditation briefing materials for selected university administrators, faculty, and staff members in the School of Education, department/program coordinators in the College of Arts and Sciences, and school district personnel. Although we had regular meetings with the accreditation team members and the Teacher Education Advisory Council members, we believed that materials packaged together would serve as a useful resource for participants during the visits. Event schedules, key facts and materials about accreditation, faculty assignments, and daily agenda were included in the notebook.

Challenge III: The Board of Examiners Visit—Putting It All Together

Forty-eight hours before the visit, the team wondered if we had addressed all issues related to the standards. As with planning for any major event, we were down to the deadline and needed to tie up any loose ends. The NCATE coordinator set up the easel and began to make the final checklist. Some of the items related to hospitality matters were elevated to the top of our agenda. For example, how should the School of Education care for its guests when they visit our campus? Has the president of the student organization recruited enough students to escort and travel with our guests? Has the transportation schedule been shared with the contracted drivers? Has the meal schedule been confirmed with the Food Service Department? Did we contact the Facility Maintenance Department to ensure that regular and scheduled maintenance in the building will occur during each day of the visit? The team worked frantically to complete these and any other last-minute details.

And finally, the moment we had all been working for arrived. Everything was in place, the building was immaculate, and faculty members and staff were ready and available to respond to any final requests from the BOE team members. All the attention to the "plan with its associated tasks" had paid off. The contributions of the faculty and staff in the School of Education were invaluable. The School of Education administrators were very grateful to our colleagues across campus and in the school district who had been available whenever we needed them. Support from the dean was a constant reassurance that we would succeed in our quest for accreditation. The faculty felt confident as we met the BOE team members on their first day on campus. And the NCATE coordinator would be forever indebted to each individual and group that participated in preparations for the accreditation visit.

Challenge IV: Reflective Analysis

On Wednesday afternoon, when the last

member of the Board of Examiners departed from the campus, the School of Education family sighed with relief. After two years of discussions and preparations for the visit, it was finally over. Only one hour earlier, the deans and department chairs had met with the BOE chairperson for the exit interview. They concluded that the School of Education had met all of the standards. We were very pleased. However, the NCATE coordinator reminded team members that while this was encouraging information, the official action would be forwarded in the spring of 1997 after the Unit Accreditation Board had met and acted on the report submitted by the Board of Examiners. Nevertheless, we still felt like celebrating. Many positive relationships among the faculty and staff members in the School of Education had been renewed.

The winter vacation arrived, but some of the accreditation team members did not depart without first discussing the five standards where weaknesses had been found that needed to be covered in our rejoinder. The NCATE coordinator met with the affected department chairperson and together they developed a plan of action for addressing the standards with weaknesses. The second semester began. The department chairperson submitted the information for the rejoinder. The final copy of the rejoinder was delivered to the NCATE office in Washington, D.C., and the waiting began.

We reflected upon our quest. The HBCU Network had helped us to revitalize our School of Education through the accreditation process—not only teacher education, but all programs leading to the preparation of school personnel. The entire school was involved in the accreditation quest. NCATE accreditation signified high quality in all of our program majors. We believed that we would achieve success in our quest because interest was high in ensuring that our programs met world-class education standards. Indeed, we felt as though we had become experts who soon would be able to assist sister HBCUs through the process. With HBCU Network support, our school experienced a sense of renewal in addressing the many kinds of teaching and learning interactions required for meeting NCATE and state accreditation standards.

In April 1997, the Unit Accreditation Board (UAB) met in Washington, D.C., to receive the Board of Examiners report. This was an intense time of waiting. Approximately two weeks after the UAB met, we finally received the official action on the accreditation of the teacher education programs in the School of Education, Howard University. Recommendations submitted by the BOE had been accepted—all standards had been met. *The School of Education's quest for NCATE accreditation had been successful.*

Reflections by Jerrie Cobb Scott

The Howard University case study walks the reader through virtually all the critical stages of the accreditation process. It describes a journey, one that begins with the preconditions and ends with the rejoinder. Between the beginning and the end are the bold forward strides and the backward slides that remind one of the typical steps needed to arrive at effective practice. The case highlights two areas of national interest, professional development schools and total quality management. The former emphasizes the importance of collaboratives between teacher education and school programs. The latter emphasizes the application of the business concepts of total quality management to educational settings. From this perspective, the Howard University case exemplifies practical applications of theories that are taught in teacher education programs. One has the feeling that we could actually change the often-cited criticism, "teachers teach the way they were taught, rather than the way they were taught to teach," into a compliment to the field of teacher education in which we are making giant steps to teach even better than we were taught to teach.

The case shows that preparation for accreditation is not a perfect process; rather, we learn from our successes and failures. While there are specific lessons embedded in the narrative, an overarching theme is that one must actually be able to apply what is learned effectively (get results) and efficiently (in a reasonable time period). For example, no matter how pressed we are for time, all faculty must be involved in the accreditation process—not a new message, but one that all too often must be learned from experience. The tendency to overrate our successes is typical, but the preparation for accreditation requires a high degree of objectivity, a stepping back to see ourselves as others see us, based on what we present. And this objectivity comes from multiple assessments, multiple perspectives, and the use of assessment results to inform change. The Howard

University case cautions us not to take lightly the complexity of change, reminding us that even after changes have been made, the requirements for consistency demand that documents accurately reflect the changes. The commitment to leave no stone unturned could well have served to reduce resistance to change. Thus, making adjustments in response to failed attempts, rather than hanging on to ineffective strategies, is difficult but ultimately required for success.

In addition to giving the reader a sense of what does not work, the case gives a sense of what does work. At least four major lessons are taught by this case.

1. Some change processes come with a price tag. An excellent example is technological upgrades. We also observe that available resources may sometimes be overlooked, such as students to assist in technology labs.

2. It is important not only to have a solid conceptual framework, but also to ensure that the multitude of colleagues within the institution, the students, and external constituents understand the framework.

3. Although assessment was an ongoing part of the process, assessment alone did not make for success. The system for continuous monitoring and reporting to stakeholders was equally important. A strategy is needed not only for preparing programs, but also for planning, monitoring, and evaluating the process of accreditation preparation.

4. An important aspect of collegiality is to take time out to celebrate successes along the way. After all, a buy-in deserves a payoff. It is possible to get so bogged down in the work that no time is left for celebration of the work and the progress. Celebration is so important that it needs to be planned for along with other important dimensions of the process.

The case suggests several questions about preparation for accreditation.

- How familiar are members of the institution with the major processes involved in accreditation, the review process, and the standards themselves? It is generally felt that each unit should worry about its own accreditation process, but we see here that the accreditation process for teacher education programs requires the involvement of external constituents such as schools.

- How does one secure commitment from the top, if it is not available? It is easy to overlook existing resources, but the Howard case demonstrates that finding areas of expertise, funding sources, and partnerships with schools can be highly beneficial to both the accreditation process and the relationships with other major players.

- To what extent do fear and resistance to change threaten the involvement of a broad-based constituency? This case illustrates that time is well spent on involving the entire community. Sometimes external consultants can be highly beneficial in breaking down barriers and simply encouraging a more cooperative agenda for all. Ultimately, though, the long-range successes are dependent upon internal commitments and involvement of a community, working together toward common goals of excellence. And this takes time.

The quest for accreditation is indeed a capstone experience, one that can be best described as a journey. The Howard University case study reminds us that this journey begins and ends with a quest for continuous quality improvements in the way we fulfill our institutional mission and in the ways we realize the most noble goals of the teacher education profession.

CHAPTER 3

Transforming the "Pass-It-On" Tradition
Xavier University of Louisiana

Loren J. Blanchard
Angela Lydon
Doris Blum

Xavier University in New Orleans, Louisiana, is the only predominantly Black Catholic university in the Western Hemisphere. Its history evolved from the nation's history. Xavier was founded because of post-Civil War conditions in the United States. The chaotic days of Reconstruction had established segregation as a way of life, and the U.S. Supreme Court's Plessy v. Ferguson decision validated this separation of the races, especially evident in the South and definitely in Louisiana. Education was profoundly affected. Inequalities existed for at least 25 years until the federal government felt a certain responsibility to its new citizens. Chiefly through the land-grant college program, it sought to provide higher education for Blacks, placing responsibility in the hands of each state legislature. Louisiana, by Act 87 passed in 1878, chartered Southern University for Colored, a land-grant college built in New Orleans.

In time, pressure from White residents forced Southern University to relocate to Scotlandville, outside of Baton Rouge, Louisiana. Through efforts of the Josephite Fathers of Baltimore and the Archbishop of New Orleans, a wealthy woman from the North brought hope to the South. Katherine Drexel (now Blessed Katherine), daughter of the millionaire Drexel banking family of Philadelphia, was persuaded to purchase the property vacated by Southern for the purpose of developing a college and university for New Orleans' Black Catholic youth. She forfeited her wealth and prestige to found a congregation of religious women, the Sisters of the Blessed Sacrament, who would commit their lives to the salvation and education of Black and Native Americans, the two most oppressed groups of her time. Katherine Drexel's presence remains at Xavier through her sisters who continue to serve there.

Despite rigid opposition, the spacious edifice that was Southern University in New Orleans was purchased in 1915 for $18,000. Also, Xavier Secondary School for Colored Students of both sexes was established. Two years later, a Teachers' Training School with a two-year curriculum was inaugurated. In 1925, it expanded into a four-year Teachers' College. Katherine Drexel's foresight in preparing teachers who would pass on spirituality, culture, knowledge, and other values to those who had nearly been smothered by ignorance and prejudice was a welcome development.

Xavier's role as an institution founded with teacher preparation as a primary goal has continued through the years. The university is still guided by its mission to provide each student with a liberal and professional education. To ensure the excellence of its programs, Xavier utilizes all relevant means, including teaching, research, and community service in a pluralistic environment, to create a more just and humane society.

The university presently continues to provide the highest standards of excellence in preparing professional educators for the 21st century. In 1997, its Division of Education trained approximately 300 professional education candidates from diverse backgrounds, at both initial and advanced program levels. The division offers Bachelor of Arts and Bachelor of Science degrees leading to Louisiana teacher certification in such fields as early childhood education, elementary education, and special education, and in art, biology, chemistry, English, health and physical education, history (social studies), mathematics, music (instrumental and vocal), and speech pathology education.

Initial program requirements include courses in general, professional, and specialized academic education, all essential to promoting teaching excellence and all leading to mastery of program outcomes related to the Education Division's conceptual framework and to teacher certification. Foundation courses provide a framework for making value judgments in education. Methods courses address individual needs and teaching specialties by exposing students and giving them experience in applying a wide variety of teaching strategies and learning theories, often through the use of advanced technology.

Other courses in the professional sequence emphasize self-concept development in relation to the role of the teacher. There also is a survey course in special education that broadens the pre-service teachers' knowledge and experience in working with individuals with exceptionalities. Carefully sequenced field experiences provide opportunities for the application of appropriate theories and techniques.

Programs at the advanced level focus on areas of curriculum and instruction, administration and supervision, and counseling—all culminating in either a master of arts degree or a master of arts in teaching degree. Scholarship, teaching, and service are integral to the advanced candidates' educational experience. The concepts of spirituality, culture, knowledge, and skills are carefully integrated into the curricula to ensure that Xavier's signature is passed on into each teacher's classroom and throughout the community.

Xavier's professional education unit looks toward the future eagerly. Its awesome challenge of preparing future professionals for excellence in their chosen occupations requires ongoing collegial reflection and dialogue on issues affecting the very existence of life and community survival in the coming millennium. Problems facing humanity range from planetary destruction to participatory governance. Professional education will have to address these concerns if it is to remain both viable and relevant.

A central task of Xavier's professional education division will be to identify appropriate coursework, frame suitable instructional strategies, and evolve meaningful field opportunities that enhance the quality of life for all. Essential to this endeavor will be ongoing instruction and training in the creative use of technology.

Xavier's professional education unit, informed and empowered by its past and cognizant of its present, recognizes that today's problems create opportunities and possibilities for envisioning a more just and humane world—a world that honors individuality, respects diversity, and acknowledges the interdependence of all beings as part of the very fabric and meaning of life itself. It is toward this end that Xavier's professional education division made the commitment to reconceptualize education through its pursuit of national accreditation by the National Council for Accreditation of Teacher Education.

Coming to Know Ourselves

The Decision. When we were initially invited to submit a proposal for a seed grant to assess our institution for NCATE readiness, we were reluctant. Our reluctance was based on memories—nearly four years past—of the arduous preparations for the Louisiana Education Department's five-year accreditation visit. Memories of collecting and searching for documentation to support various standards, setting up meetings to apprise administrators of the types of questions to expect from visiting team members, holding writing sessions with faculty members that lasted until the wee hours of the morning, experiencing power failures that resulted in near cardiac arrests as we forgot to hit the "save" key—all led us to think that our department was not ready to prepare for national accreditation—which would surely prove to be more rigorous than our state preparations.

Our department launched an independent initiative, the Teacher Education Reform Initiative, to examine our teacher preparation program's response to current classroom issues. We recognized that some of our program weaknesses (identified through surveying nearly 1,200 individuals, including Xavier pre-service and in-service teachers, principals, counselors, and other education stakeholders in the community, and through use of external evaluators) were areas in which NCATE expected more readiness. These program weaknesses centered on technology, inclusive education, behavioral management training emphasizing conflict resolution skills, the need to merge undergraduate and graduate teacher education programs, and the lack of a unified conceptual framework that undergirded all teacher education curricula and instruction.

Xavier is one of the historically Black colleges and universities that sought Mott Foundation funding to prepare for NCATE accreditation via an accelerated mentoring program. We were assigned a lead consultant whose role was to offer technical support to our preparation.

Internal Assessment: The "Tremor". The first step of our NCATE quest was to inform all relevant university parties of our intent to secure national accreditation for our teacher education program. During this time, the NCATE Coordinating Committee (three Education Division members) scheduled information meetings for both university leadership and Secondary Education Council members to learn the multiple intricacies of the NCATE process. Attendance at these meetings was, at best, sparse, and the NCATE Coordinating Committee began to realize that organizing one's cohorts was, in and of itself, tricky. Accompanied by a memorandum explaining NCATE was a copy of the needs assessment instrument, which each recipient was asked to complete and return within one week.

Amid an array of excuses as to why various faculty and a few university administrators felt it inappropriate to be asked to complete such a rating scale, the NCATE Coordinating Committee, representing both undergraduate and graduate programs, calculated the mean scores for each of the assessment indicators. The Xavier community appeared to have inflated impressions about the quality of the teacher education program. The Coordinating Committee collected documentation on the NCATE standards to prepare our preconditions self-study. At this time, the documentation of the Teacher Education Division began.

HBCU Network Assessment: The Earthquake. Concurrent with preparing the self-report came the first real "NCATE tremor," which occurred as the Coordinating Committee asked key individuals to prepare program review documents for their various teacher education disciplines—in compliance with respective learned society guidelines. The tremor was so jolting that the committee postponed the request and allowed it to be recognized as a weakness during the Technical Support Network's on-site visit in December 1995.

When the report was completed and the schedule for the on-site visit was finalized in consultation with our Network mentor, four team members came to our campus to determine and report on whether our perceptions of our teacher education program were commensurate with NCATE's. By the time the network team members had concluded their three-day meeting and writing sessions and all of Xavier's teacher education program stakeholders (from the university president to the department secretary) gathered around the table to learn of the team members' findings, the second tremor had already hit. This time, however, the tremor grew to earthquake proportions.

It was as if the department's 50-plus-year foundation began to crumble as we learned that the team members' ratings agreed with only 7 of the 25 indicators on the needs assessment completed by the Network consultants. All the other indicators were overrated by the Xavier professional education community when compared with the Network team's ratings. We learned that our governance structure had to be reorganized and that our undergraduate and graduate teacher education programs had to be under one umbrella. We learned that our 50-plus-year teacher education program had no identifiable, well-documented conceptual framework. We learned that our undergraduate and graduate departments had no documented (or conceptualized) plan for recruiting and retaining a diverse student body and faculty. We learned that our teacher education programs should have one person responsible for placing and supervising 18 student teachers as a full-time load. This was contrary to our faculty handbook's current policy of 36 student teachers constituting a full-time load. We learned that the infusion of technology had to be evidenced in every course across our teacher education programs. We learned that program review documents had to be completed for each of the 12 programs and submitted to the respective learned societies for evaluation. As the network team prepared to leave, it appeared that the Xavier community recognized them as messengers of doom! However, the accreditation earthquake quickly shook us into action.

Repairing Ourselves

Overcoming the Identity Crisis. Within one week of the Network team's departure, we reconvened the Xavier group who participated in the exit report meeting. We wanted to give the professional education community an opportunity to flesh out their reactions to the findings within a structured forum. Although various issues were raised, one resounding question continued to surface: How do we respond to NCATE standards without compromising the historic mission and uniqueness of our institution? Xavier University is the only institution in the United States that is both historically Black and Catholic. Xavier strives to combine the best attributes of both its faith and its culture to prepare its students to assume leadership roles in society. Such a distinction, the group felt, could not be replaced or overshadowed by NCATE standards. We decided to continue with the second phase of the HBCU Network model, the educative phase.

Entering the Educative Phase. Xavier's NCATE Coordinating Team developed a plan to respond to recommendations made by both the Network team and our professional community. Subcommittees addressed each recommendation with a proposed time frame. Each subcommittee meeting was documented and submitted to the subcommittee responsible for developing the living documents room. At this point, we began to address our cited weaknesses, starting with the program standards. Concurrently, we enlisted the expertise of our Network consultant.

Using Technical Support. Originally, our understanding of the role of the mentor was that this person would provide technical support throughout the entire NCATE preparation process.

Finding the right match between our institution and the mentor was essential to its success. Mutual respect, trust, availability, consistent and meaningful communication, as well as an understanding of the uniqueness of the institution are the ingredients of a good Xavier "gumbo." If any of these ingredients is missing, the gumbo is spoiled. New Orleans chefs know that it is difficult to make a good gumbo on the first try—so, too, with the mentoring process. The first try, delicious as it was, needed a more savory mixture of Xavier's ingredients: respect, trust, availability, communication, and a more robust understanding of our institutional uniqueness. A new chef-mentor assisted us in achieving the perfect blend of seasonings.

Confronting the Folio Fear. Because we had been given an extended deadline to submit our responses to professional association guidelines, it became important for the various programs to complete the work as quickly as possible. The members of the NCATE Coordinating Committee met with each person responsible for development of program standards documents, explaining the purpose and the procedures to be followed. All expressed concern about the amount of work and the time constraints placed on an already overworked faculty. Nonetheless, the task was accepted with goodwill. Most faculty members felt that writing the responses was a true learning experience. It became evident, however, that more learning was needed when all of the documents were returned labeled not in compliance with the learned societies' standards. The next question arose: should we, would we, prepare rejoinders?

Naturally, those who had spent so much time on the originals were reluctant to do them again, and this time within even greater time restraints. After consulting with our mentor, we agreed that for the good of the whole NCATE process, we would send in the rejoinders. They were completed within the timeline and resubmitted. With only two months to go before our mock visit, though, we still awaited final approval.

Unleashing the Energy to Change

Restructuring Governance. As indicated earlier, one of the Network's recommendations was to seriously consider reorganizing and restructuring our undergraduate and graduate teacher education programs into a single unit with a single unit head. Before this recommendation, the undergraduate and graduate areas functioned independently rather than interdependently. This situation often resulted in duplications in coursework and textbook selection, misunderstanding of curricular offerings across programs, and a dearth of intellectual discourse among faculty responsible for the teacher education programs.

In response to the NCATE mandate for a single governance unit, the university president established an ad hoc committee consisting of the academic vice president, the dean of Arts and Sciences, the dean of the Graduate Division, the chairperson of the Undergraduate Division, and a faculty representative from both graduate and undergraduate programs. A variety of models were examined for possible adoption, but none seemed to fit our specific needs, background, and history.

Eventually, the administration chose a model that provided for a Division of Education. The entire division, both the undergraduate and graduate programs, is housed in the College of Arts and Sciences and reports directly to the dean of the college. This unit is headed by a director who chooses two faculty members to act as assistants—one from the undergraduate program and one from the graduate program. Three faculty committees were established: an undergraduate committee, a graduate committee, and a joint faculty committee that developed and implemented academic policies and procedures for the unit.

The Division of Education is strongly committed to expanding and supporting a professional partnership of university-based educators with professionals in public and private school systems. Hence, the division established the Professional Advisory Council to obtain feedback from the professional community of educators in the local and regional areas. This group of educators advises the division on the following matters: 1) field experiences and practice teaching opportunities for our students; 2) curriculum considerations to enhance the division's learner outcomes; 3) feedback from the community on the division's role in K-12 schools; 4) positioning the division for the future of teacher education in the city, region/state, and nation.

The reorganization plan was approved by Xavier's Board of Trustees for implementation in the fall 1996 semester. In accordance with the new governance model, undergraduate, graduate, and secondary education faculty began regular joint meetings—the collaboration of a collegial community. The meeting topics often focused on NCATE standards. Simultaneously, faculty members began to learn more about one another, both professionally and personally. This became particularly valuable in forming various subcommittees that could work together in fulfilling the goals of the educative plan.

Reframing the Conceptual Model. "Framing" the conceptual framework has indeed been a challenge and a chore, because the framework is the rudder that steers the entire ship of NCATE. Part of the process of developing the conceptual framework involved grappling with the core concepts, knowledge base, and assessment and evaluation components. To facilitate development of the conceptual framework, professional clinics were scheduled and conducted by an HBCU Network consultant. During the clinics, professional education faculty came to grips with the complexities that surround the parameters of the first standard for the NCATE institutional report.

Envisioning a graphic that would express Xavier's unique heritage, as well as speak to the dynamic vision needed for teacher education in the new millennium, was indeed a formidable task. As the unit sought educational renewal (Goodlad, 1991), the group became reflective practitioners (Schoen, 1997) who listened to each other, interacted with each other, and asked probing questions in an ever-widening circle of inquiry. Gradually the conceptual framework evolved.

The conceptual framework of the initial and advanced professional education division can be visualized as a spiral of interrelated yet differentiated concepts for living, growing, teaching, and learning. The organizing theme, *Pass It On: Educating for Unity and Community through Spirituality, Diversity and Intellectual Vitality*, crystallizes the assumptions and beliefs that Xavier's professional education unit brings to all teaching and learning. The unit recognizes its responsibility to infuse all professional education faculty with the ability to recognize and develop the gifts and rich heritage that each person brings to the program. At the same time, unfolding in each student is the ability to "pass it on" by living in unity and community with a commitment to spirituality, diversity, and intellectual vitality. As part of its conceptual framework, the unit acknowledges the university's historic heritage as a Black Catholic institution and utilizes the varied experiences of a diverse faculty and the literature of the professional education field as guides in the integration of the stated values of a professional education within a liberal arts curriculum.

The unit's curriculum identifies five core elements—values, culture, spirituality, knowledge, and skills—which, when linked to the knowledge base and assessment strategies, constitute the conceptual framework for the Division of Education. Each student entering Xavier's professional education program already manifests these elements to some degree. The function of the unit, therefore, is to weave a pattern so that the students' acquisition of the core elements will be enhanced as they integrate them more fully into their personal lives. In this way, their professional practice also can reflect and model these same core elements.

The above concepts are supported and strengthened by four integral processes that guide the Xavier University teaching and learning experience: reflection, relationality, inquiry, and interaction. These are essential components of the program as a whole, and when connected to the conceptual underpinnings of the professional education unit, they identify how knowledge is acquired and how practice is initiated and delivered.

The faculty recognizes that the five elements and four processes embrace all life, all peoples, and all cultures, and the concepts and processes affirm that the Xavier community is part of a larger world. Xavier University's mission statement supports this vision in that it challenges and, at the same time, empowers its students and faculty to embrace the entire global community in the human struggle to create and establish a more just and humane society. This understanding fosters inclusion rather than exclusion. It elicits ongoing emancipatory action, which in turn informs all teaching and learning at Xavier University. As such, the five core elements and the four integral processes affirm the sacredness of all life.

Revitalizing the "Pass-It-On" Tradition

Reaffirming Our Mission. Dr. Norman C. Francis, president of Xavier University, has reaffirmed his commitment to national standards of excellence for the improvement of education.

This includes his commitment to the NCATE initiative as Xavier's means of fulfilling its mission to the education of America's youth. He has addressed the academic community of Xavier on several occasions encouraging efforts of the new Division of Education to secure NCATE acceptance. He has stated that his goal is to have programs in education achieve the national recognition and status that Xavier's science programs have achieved. Francis' charge to the academic community as a whole has centered around the question, "When was the last time you told a student, 'I think you're good enough to be a teacher?'" Such a question is grounded in his belief that Xavier should be recruiting among "the best and the brightest" to relieve shortages of quality minority teachers.

Xavier's professional education faculty also recognizes the need to revitalize and recommit the university to training exemplary pre-service and advanced candidates for the teaching profession. For the past three years, the teacher education faculty has re-examined both the initial and advanced programs, and it is well on its way to forming a unified Division that has as its mission a teacher education program designed for successful classroom practice in the 21st century.

Committing to Collegiality and Collaboration. From the beginning of the initiative, the faculty has worked to achieve the end goal of NCATE approval. Initially, not everyone was in favor, but no one refused any task, and all participated in laborious assignments and committee work. One could almost feel fusion taking place. Old friends worked together again, and new relationships were formed as discussion and sharing took place at our divisional meetings. Physical and program separation began to decrease as we recognized the importance of each person to the entire process.

The three faculty members who serve as the NCATE Coordinating Team bonded, and each added his or her particular talents to the whole. Having three people responsible for the progress of our NCATE preparations worked well for us, as we supported each other, calming, energizing, crying, or laughing together. We would never have bonded without the collective labor of all. Some even accepted summer assignments to assure that we would be that much further ahead in the fall, the semester of our actual NCATE visit.

Reenvisioning the Accreditation Process. As we look forward to the completion of the NCATE initiative, we are encouraged by the words of President Francis, who implied at our mock NCATE accreditation visit that Xavier saw the Division of Education as a vital, expanding entity of the university. To us, the division faculty's completion of the process brings teacher education full cycle, because Xavier was founded as a teacher training institution.

The move toward NCATE accreditation by the professional education faculty at Xavier University has been ongoing, steady, and determined. Setting priorities, the Coordinating Committee had dug in its heels to tackle both the big and the small issues that need to be addressed before the arrival of the Board of Examiners (BOE) team. But it was the willingness and participation of the professional education faculty that made all the difference and that enabled us as a unit to pass on to the BOE team the visions and dreams of Xavier University's teacher education program.

The Pre-Visit: Final Planning and Preparation for Passing on the Tradition

NCATE preparation placed us in a state of continual planning and anticipation. First, there was the pre-assessment visit. With the results of the pre-assessment visit in hand, we began planning for the mock visit. The mock visit was strategically planned six months before the BOE visit. After the mock visit, the Xavier Coordinating Committee worked frantically to finalize the institutional report, revise the Division of Education handbooks, and organize the living documents facility for the pre-visit of the BOE team chair. Resolutely forging their way forward, with numerous calls to the team chair, the Coordinating Committee devised an agenda that allowed ample time for the division chair, Coordinating Committee, and education faculty to meet. Into the wee hours before the pre-visit, the Coordinating Committee combed 20 drawers of files, so that the team chair would find few or no discrepancies in documentation. The room provided evidence that reflected Xavier's Division of Education. The Coordinating Committee was certain of the unit's preparedness.

A Coordinating Committee member met the team chair at the airport. It felt good to be able to match a face with a voice (and the mind behind countless electronic messages). We arrived on campus a little after the noon hour and began working through the agenda. The Coordinating Committee had set aside a large block of time for review of the living agenda. To our surprise (and, perhaps, dismay), our team chair spent no longer than 15 minutes with the documents and then reported, "Everything is fine!" One perplexed committee member retorted, "Are you sure?" The chair assured us that everything was in order and that the pre-visit was not designed to review the documents file by file. Rather, it was to educate the unit on the processes used during the BOE visit. Our meeting evolved into intense question-and-answer sessions. The most fruitful meeting for the Coordinating Committee was the joint planning session for the entire BOE visit. The planning was specific and detailed. By the end of the meeting, we knew exactly what would occur each of the five days, down to the very second.

The team chair, having completed 15 prior BOE visits, shared much of her vast reservoir of NCATE knowledge with the Coordinating Committee. As we attentively listened to her BOE accounts, the Coordinating Committee was able to glean those areas (not directly identified during our pre-visit) that still needed some finishing touches. As we had intuitively sensed the pre-visit to be a draining experience, we somehow felt that at the end of our team chair's intense one-and-a-half-day period with us, she boarded the plane feeling relatively lifeless. For we had siphoned all the knowledge from her that we possibly could to guarantee our readiness for the BOE visit.

We were now poised for the final six weeks! Before the dawning of October 25, 1997, when the

BOE would arrive on Xavier University's campus, we had much to accomplish. The Coordinating Committee devised strategies for every detail of the coming six-week period. The majority of this time was spent educating and informing numerous publics about Xavier's conceptual framework and its relevance to the larger school community. More frequent meetings were also held within the university community.

A great deal of energy and time went into planning the itinerary for the BOE team members both on and off campus, to make their stay in "the city that care forgot" memorable. The Coordinating Committee made final preparations for setting up the suite of rooms that would house the living documents, meeting areas, and hospitality. Not a moment was wasted during this interval, and when the day finally loomed, the Coordinating Committee knew that it had accomplished all that it had planned for a smooth and successful BOE visit.

The BOE Team Visit: The Declaration of the "Passing-It-On" Tradition

As is typical in New Orleans, a major conference attempted to sabotage our first meeting with the BOE team. Two hours late, four BOE team members finally arrived on campus. When the first session finally started, introductions were made and a general orientation to the NCATE suite was given to the BOE members and the Louisiana State Department of Education representative (also a member of the NCATE team). The NCATE agenda template we used was invaluable in that it facilitated the BOE's opportunity to put in context what the Division of Education documented in its institutional report.

A nervous, exhausted Coordinating Committee gathered with university officials for the exit report. We had an idea of the outcome because we had been kept informed of the BOE's concerns. However, we were not about to exhale until we actually heard and saw the results. Two areas of weakness were noted by the BOE team—student diversity and library resources. All the other standards were met!

With a sigh of delighted relief, we concluded our BOE visit. Our two-year saga toward national accreditation had come closer to fulfillment. The tired triumvirate (the Coordinating Committee) could almost resume a normal collegiate existence, after they completed a rejoinder to the BOE final report.

We have now concluded the last stage in our journey toward NCATE accreditation. This final juncture would not have been possible without the support, encouragement, and care of the HBCU Technical Support Network. The mission of the Network to assist HBCUs in the successful completion of NCATE accreditation came to fruition at Xavier University of Louisiana. A small, historically Black and Catholic university, in the crescent bend of the Mississippi, achieved its goal of becoming a part of the NCATE community.

Xavier University was accredited in March 1998.

Reflections by Kay L. Hegler

Reenvisioning the Accreditation Process

As the consultants looked forward to the completion of the NCATE initiative, we were encouraged by the words of President Francis who implied at our mock NCATE visit that Xavier saw the Division of Education as a vital, expanding entity of the university. To us, the division faculty, the completion of the process brought the place of teacher education full circle, because Xavier was founded as a teacher training institution. The move toward NCATE accreditation by the professional education faculty at Xavier University had been ongoing, steady, and determined. Setting priorities, the Coordinating Committee "dug in" its heels to tackle both the big and small issues that needed to be addressed before the arrival of the BOE team. But it was the willingness and participation of the professional education faculty that made all the difference and enabled the unit to pass on to the BOE team the dream-vision of Xavier University's teacher education program.

The consultants felt that the university's process illustrated that change is indeed a process. We were able to make several observations about the accreditation process.

- On some points, the unit head and university administrators repeatedly heard recommendations for change to more adequately meet the standards of quality established by NCATE. The consultant team made one needs assessment visit; an individual HBCU consultant outside of the HBCUTSN team was on campus twice; the HBCUTSN lead consultant was on campus once without a team; and a mock team visited the institution. These five consultancies occurred over the course of approximately 19 months. For example, faculty load remained an area of concern although this had been identified in each of the visits. The institution would have appeared to be more responsive if change had been completed earlier in the process.

- All faculty and especially the coordinating committee members expended large portions of summer and weekend time to complete the process; they received minimally adequate compensation for the arduous task.

- A stable, capable, and committed team of three respected faculty served as the NCATE coordinating committee. Although a different faculty member served as Unit Head during each of the three years of preparation for NCATE review, this coordinating committee established goals and maintained momentum between consultant visits.

- The unit exists within the structure of a financially stable university and has excellent support from administrators. These campus leaders listened to the consistent reports of several consultants and were willing to make changes according to the concerns noted by the consultants.

- The university housed the initial programs in the newly constructed library and classroom facility and made plans to house the advanced programs in this exemplary facility by the time of the actual NCATE review.

- The unit faculty were responsive to guidance offered by the consultants. Faculty members attended long meetings, generated their own ideas, used effective communication skills, and developed a unique conceptual framework appropriate to Xavier.

- The unit is housed in a building with modern technology and individual faculty members are obtaining in-service education for classroom applications.

- The unit faculty developed a strong conceptual framework and a model of this framework. The faculty revised course syllabi to enhance the implementation and articulation of this conceptual framework.

CHAPTER 4

WEAVING OUTCOMES INTO THE FABRIC OF THE PROGRAM

DELAWARE STATE UNIVERSITY

Aleta M. Hannah
Charles M. Hodge
Johnny Tolliver

Delaware State University is a comprehensive, public, land-grant institution that offers baccalaureate and master's degrees. Delaware State was established by the Delaware General Assembly in 1891 as an institution of higher learning (high school) for colored students in agriculture and mechanical arts. After a reorganization of its academic programs into five divisions—education and psychology, natural sciences and mathematics, languages and literature, social sciences, and vocational education—the institution was renamed Delaware State College in 1948. The institution was renamed Delaware State University in 1993 when it was reorganized into schools. The academic programs at Delaware State University are offered through one college (Arts and Sciences) and three schools (Agriculture, Natural Resources, and Family and Consumer Sciences; Education and Professional Studies; and Management). The college and three schools offer 30 baccalaureate degrees with 73 options and 12 master's degrees. Twenty-eight options are offered in the undergraduate teacher education program. The Education Department established the first graduate program, Curriculum and Instruction, in 1981. Other master's degree programs in education are Biology, Physics, Special Education, Science Education, and Adult Literacy and Basic Education. In 1998, the Department of Education was accredited by NCATE, and individual teacher education programs have been approved by respective specialty organizations. Delaware State University is accredited by the Middle States Association of Colleges and Schools.

Located in Dover, Delaware's capital city, the university's mission is to provide citizens of the state, and others who are admitted, a meaningful and relevant education that emphasizes both liberal studies and preparation for professional careers. In accordance with its heritage, the university serves a diverse student population with a broad range of programs and promotes the belief that preparing students to be competitive in a global society is a continuing challenge that is best fostered in a multicultural learning environment. A special challenge for the university is to prepare minority students for career pursuits in those areas where they have been traditionally and historically underrepresented. Delaware State University emphasizes instruction, service, and research as a means of preparing graduates who are competent, productive, and contributing citizens. In pursuit of fulfilling its mission, the university places an emphasis on quality teaching and concurrently stresses the faculty's obligation to engage in research that can add to the body of knowledge leading to the solution of the problems that confront the regional, national and world communities.

This case study is designed to help other HBCUs understand the upward climb toward meeting the national standards for teacher education programs. Weaving the NCATE outcomes into the fabric of the Teacher Education Program has proven to be an enlightening and enhancing experience for individuals and for the program. Three major hurdles evolved during the process of preparing for accreditation: Leadership, Education, and Collaboration. As with any institution, leadership is key to success, especially when the goal is as complex and important as attaining accreditation. Education, knowledge about the tasks to achieve the desired goal, is a necessary component for success. And, in the case of accreditation, collaboration becomes the thread that weaves NCATE standards into the fabric of the program.

Leadership

Consistent and persistent leadership is needed to support the accreditation initiative, making leadership an important strand in weaving NCATE outcomes into the fabric of the program. The administration, faculty, staff, students, and professional community at Delaware State University have systematically upgraded its teacher education program. This process was partially evident during the late 1980s and early 1990s leading up to the attempt to seek NCATE accreditation in 1995. For instance, in 1987-88, the chair brought several national speakers (e.g. Asa Hilliard, Herbert Kohl, Asanti Molefi, and Nancy Zimpher) to campus to build a foundation for developing the knowledge base for our program. Attendance at these events was practically nonexistent. One of the lessons learned was that this approach has limited pay-offs if it is not grounded in a clear understanding of what a knowledge base is and how one uses a knowledge base to design programs.

In 1989, a permanent chair was hired. The new chair picked up the NCATE charge and took a series of actions toward NCATE accreditation. These initial actions included reviewing other accredited programs, e.g., several key players visited Bowie State University to learn firsthand about their accreditation experiences, and arranging a visit from an NCATE consultant. In 1992, a thread of hope began to weave itself throughout the program as the first visible movement toward NCATE accreditation materialized. The chair took steps to procure Title III funds to support various NCATE preparation efforts. University leadership took a more serious interest in improving the teacher education program and preparing for NCATE accreditation. In 1993, a budget was established and an NCATE coordinator was hired to lead the university through the NCATE accreditation process. The coordinator began to read the NCATE documents, meet with faculty of the undergraduate teacher education programs, assign faculty to take a lead in developing program folios, and interact with administrators.

Gaining a grant from NCATE offered another thread for weaving the NCATE outcomes into the fabric of the program. The grant enabled Delaware State University to join the Historically Black Colleges and Universities Teacher Education Technical Support Network (HBCUTSN) administered by AACTE and NCATE. The Network provided valuable support to professional education units by assisting administrators, faculty, and staff in strengthening teacher preparation programs and in readying themselves for the NCATE accreditation process. Also, the vice president for academic affairs and the chair of the Department of Education attended an HBCU Technical Support Network Orientation meeting on August 12-14, 1995, in San Francisco. The meeting provided an introduction to technical assistance offered under the grant. Importantly too, the meeting made it immensely clear that all sectors of the university, not just administrators, would need to educate themselves about the process and work together to get the job done. Upon their return, the vice president for academic affairs and the head of the Professional Education Unit began a rigorous attempt to inform the university at large about NCATE. Through general faculty/staff meetings and the Teacher Education Council, the various components of the needs assessment instrument were discussed. A Steering Committee was established, and self-assessment data were collected for the first phase of our work. Prompted by the efforts to conduct a self-assessment as part of phase one of the HBCUTSN Needs Assessment, we were beginning to move in a more conscious way toward educating ourselves about the NCATE process and committing ourselves to a collaborative process. The lesson here was that education and collaboration must move bi-directionally between the administrators and the members of the unit.

Education

To show how the thread of weaving NCATE standards into the fabric of the education program, this section uses the reflective hindsight of the co-chair of the NCATE committee. It is hoped that this section will shed some light on the types of questions that should be asked early in the process. As stated in the notes of the co-chair, "I am now learning to become a visionary, a planner, a leader, a collaborator, an evaluator and statistician who goes beyond the narrow scope of my chosen area of study to a wider scope of education as a multifaceted profession." Three dimensions of the NCATE experience are treated here from the perspective of a co-chair: acquiring knowledge of the process, understanding how to develop a conceptual framework, and becoming knowledgeable of the requirements for joint State/NCATE partnerships.

Acquiring Knowledge. It has become apparent that all too often, the person who is assigned to take a lead role in the NCATE process is thought to be responsible for acquiring knowledge of the process. In hindsight, the co-chair of the process views the communication to all members of the university family as one of the first steps in the process. Given the opportunity for a repeat performance, she would: 1) jumpstart the NCATE process with a campus-wide campaign in an all-day general assembly; 2) invite NCATE officials or consultants to give a facsimile of the annual NCATE orientation for faculty; 3) engage in a rigorous self-assessment followed by an external assessment; and 4) share the results of the assessment with a broad spectrum of the university family, particularly the faculty persons who will be responsible for further program development and NCATE preparation. It will be noted that some of these efforts did take place, but the point here is that their implementation should be foresight instead of hindsight.

Conceptual Framework. Another point of importance that our co-chair acknowledged was that her willingness to work hard and learn was not enough: "Beginning with a review of the NCATE manuals really was just that—a beginning point. . . When I attended the American Association of Colleges for Teacher Education (AACTE) conference, the new knowledge gained left me impressed, overwhelmed, challenged, dumbfounded, and even scared, as the tasks ahead were mammoth." Regarding the Conceptual Framework, it was clear that it should represent what we believed our teachers should know and be able to do, but, says the co-chair, other critical questions must be raised. "How do a conceptual framework and a knowledge base differ? How does one incorporate what teachers should know and be able to do into the program? How is this framework made coherent and consistent throughout the teacher education program?" On the backdrop of the conceptual framework, other areas of knowledge make more sense—NCATE Standards, Preconditions, Institutional Reports, Professional Clinics, and the Document Room.

NCATE/State Partnerships. In its beginning stages of development, the issue of joint NCATE/State Partnerships surfaced time and time again at the AACTE conference. We learned that NCATE coordinators should be aware of the conditions of such agreements.

At the AACTE meeting, I was made aware that Delaware was a partnership state. What did this mean? What were the ramifications of this agreement? ...During the fall of 1996, we began to feel the effects of the joint partnership between NCATE and the State of Delaware as we sat through orientation meetings with representatives from all four higher education institutions within the State. The partnership option that the State chose was to have concurrent visits by two separate teams in which the state applies state standards to programs and the NCATE team applies NCATE standards. Even though we all sat through the meetings, it did not dawn on us that two separate reviews were to take place and would at first overshadow the promise that a partnership would make accreditation/certification an easier process for institutions. . . . Because DSU was the first institution to apply for accreditation/certification, the details of the partnership were still evolving. Consequently, we felt like a test-case for the Joint Partnership.

Change is a dynamic aspect of growth. More important than being perceived as a test-case is knowing in advance that an institution may enter the accreditation process during the early phase of an externally-based change initiative. Most likely, the change will eventually yield positive results, but the benefits will come partially through trial-and-error practices in implementation. It is important for NCATE coordinators to know as much as possible about the particularities of changes that are being initiated and to take steps to limit the potential negative effects that such changes may have on the preparation for accreditation.

Collaboration

Assessment. The HBCUTSN Needs Assessment team visited the campus and conducted the needs assessment review on October 13-15, 1996. Feedback from this team proved to be highly valuable in enhancing the teacher preparation programs and in structuring the university's quest for national accreditation. This visit was the teacher education program's most extensive and intense exposure to NCATE standards and the impact these standards have on the quality of teacher education programs and faculty. The Network Team's evaluation of the teacher education program covered seven areas: High Quality, Conceptual Framework, Diversity, Intellectual Vitality, Technology, Collaboration, and Evaluation and Assessment. The HBCUTSN Team gave oral and written feedback relative to these seven areas. Both general information and specific concerns and recommendations were addressed. As a result of the feedback, an NCATE Steering Committee at Delaware State revisited areas of concern, setting in motion a series of much needed collaborative efforts. The Steering Committee drew faculty participation and collaboration from across the campus to participate in the quest for national accreditation.

Governance. Areas of change for the teacher education program first recommended pinpointing a single individual, the chairperson of the Department of Education, as head of the Professional Education Unit. Secondly, a coordinator was selected from the Department of Education to coordinate all teacher education programs located outside the Department of Education. Teacher education programs housed in the Department of Education within the School of Education and Professional Studies, as well as those located in the School of Agriculture, Natural Resources, and Family and Consumer Sciences; the School of Management; and the College of Arts and

Sciences were included, as well. Utilizing a coordinator in this fashion enhanced collaboration between the Department of Education and other departments representing content areas.

The restructuring of the Professional Education Unit meant that the organizational chart needed to be revamped. Roles of the dean of Education and Professional Studies; the dean of Research, Continuing Education, and Graduate Studies; the chairperson of the Department of Education; the Teacher Education Council; and the Graduate Council were clarified. A delineation was made between the governance of the Teacher Education Council (a policy advisory and appeals body) and its relationship to the Department of Education.

A close analysis of the teacher education program stimulated further restructuring of the Department of Education. Program coordinators for Elementary Education, Special Education, and Secondary Education were added. The restructuring of the Department of Education was a major step toward shared decision-making within the Department. Academic and administrative duties of the 12 teacher education programs within the Department of Education are now shared among these coordinators. The content area coordinator coordinates the programs outside the Department of Education. The program coordinators provide leadership, guide the response for the specialty professional organization program reviews, provide cohesiveness across programs, assist in revising of syllabi to include program outcomes, and assist with other activities as needed.

Unit Activities. The Department of Education was given the leadership and administrative responsibility for the Professional Education Unit. The Department began to set goals focused on defining and describing the knowledge bases of the conceptual framework. The Department revisited its existing goals and redefined them to meet the needs of a diverse population of students for the 21st century. Members of the Professional Education Unit and teacher educators within and outside the Department of Education conducted research on "best practices" relative to the goals. A two-day retreat was held in February 1997 to discuss the findings and incorporate them into the teacher education program. The retreat brought consensus on other aspects of the conceptual framework. A Network consultant assisted in this process.

As part of the conceptual framework, the Department created an acronym, CITATED, to represent outcomes for teacher candidates set by the teacher educators at the retreat. The acronym, was used to aid the retention of the following goals and outcomes: C = Content and Pedagogical Knowledge, I = Interpersonal Skills, T = Theories of Teaching and Learning, A = Assessment, T = Technology, E = Effective Teaching Skills, D = Diversity. These outcomes were woven into the courses taught in the teacher education program by collaborative teams.

Additionally, the Professional Education Unit's standards were cross-referenced with those of NCATE as well as state standards and those of specialty area professional organizations. A subcommittee of the Professional Education Unit checked the syllabi of each teacher education program for relevant objectives, content, teaching methodology, student roles, assessments, and resources. The Professional Education Unit's conceptual framework was integrated throughout the teacher education program through this process.

Other educational activities leading toward national accreditation were occurring concurrently. The head of the Professional Education Unit and the chair of Category I attended the HBCUTSN Winter Seminar of February 21, 1996, in Chicago. Seminar materials and reports were disseminated among the faculty at large through small group sessions and departmental meetings. Committees were formed that addressed the governance structure, knowledge bases, and the articulation of a conceptual framework. A large group met weekly to discuss progress of the national accreditation quest; these included the Steering Committee, composed of the provost and dean of Academic Affairs, dean of Arts and Sciences, dean of Education and Professional Studies, NCATE campus coordinator, the unit head, all category chairs, assistant vice president for instructional support, head librarian, and director of public relations.

An official NCATE accreditation kick-off meeting and work session occurred on March 9, 1996. Members of the Professional Education unit, the University at large, the local and state agencies, as well as the broader community engaged in an all day session where the purpose, time lines, definition, scope and significance of NCATE accreditation were thoroughly reviewed and explained. Considerable discussion and debate relative to the components of the conceptual framework at Delaware State University occurred during the work sessions. Unit faculty proposed various conceptual models. Ultimately a space shuttle was selected as the conceptual model. The space shuttle depicts the journey of the candidate at entry and his/her progress through the various stages of matriculation for degree completion. Additionally, unit members discussed and proposed three themes. These themes were assigned to the Steering Committee for final review, resulting in the adoption of the theme "Effective Teachers within Diverse Populations for the 21st Century."

During the spring and summer of 1996, program materials were prepared for NCATE and NASDTEC review by departments housing teacher education programs. Responses to program guidelines were submitted for review to their respective state and professional associations in August 1997 for those programs that had not previously met the standards of their professional associations.

Concurrently, preparations for the institutional report occurred during the fall, spring, and summer of 1996 and 1997. The Category I Committee conducted workshops to ensure that all elements of the conceptual framework were incorporated into the teacher education curriculum. Data were collected describing the unit faculty, students, and governance structure in preparation for the institutional self-study report. The Professional Education Unit and the Steering Committee conducted continuous "brown bag" luncheons and departmental seminars. NCATE topics involving the organizing themes and the

NCATE/NASDTEC standards were presented to the faculty, students, staff, and the broader community.

Committees of campus and community educators and students met to develop plans so that the teacher education program would function in a smooth and coordinated manner. Technology, diversity, and assessment plans were developed. The Technology Plan includes goals for increasing candidates' basic computer skills in word processing, database management, and spreadsheet development as well as use of the Internet and World Wide Web for information searches. The Technology Plan also includes the development of a comprehensive learning center that is located in the William C. Jason Library. A full-time staff member with training and experience in technology utilization and instruction was hired to direct the technology program.

The Diversity Plan for the Professional Education Unit was developed around the goal of recruiting and retaining candidates from culturally diverse backgrounds. Additionally, the Diversity Plan included a request for funds from the president of the university to recruit foreign students, Hispanics, and Blacks into the teacher education programs. Scholarships were identified in the various departments that house teacher education programs. Scholarships for minorities and students from low socioeconomic backgrounds as well as scholarships for students with disabilities were targeted as part of the plan.

Components of the Professional Education Unit's Assessment Plan included the development of a PRAXIS I plan, the revision of the teacher education program regulations, the development of a teacher education candidate success plan, and the development of a candidate database. The assessment plan also included hiring a director of student support services in December 1997. Responsibilities of this new position include monitoring the admission, matriculation, and exit requirements of the students in the teacher education program. The PRAXIS I plan and the candidate success plan set forth remedial procedures to be followed if a candidate is not meeting GPA and other requirements.

Reweaving for Better Outcomes. A second retreat was held on the campus in May 1997. Department of Education faculty as well as faculty from content areas, teacher education majors, and public school educators attended the retreat. The conceptual frame-work with its knowledge bases, assessment plan, diversity plan, and technology plan were thoroughly discussed and redefined. Once completed, we arranged for a mock review by the HBCU network. The mock team visited the campus from September 13-16, 1997, and conducted a review of the professional teacher preparation program. The mock team provided valuable insight and advice concerning the governance structure, conceptual framework's knowledge base and field experiences. More specifically, the recommendations included revising and updating documents to reflect more accurately the current responsibilities of the Teacher Education Council, infusing the conceptual framework more thoroughly into the teacher education program, and specifying more concisely the progressive levels of the field experience component. The team also recommended that the location of the Exhibit Room be moved to a location with a larger space and that care be given to clarifying documentation in the institutional report. Lastly, the mock team advised the administration relative to the feasibility of continuing the process or engaging in further preparation prior to submitting its institutional report for the office visit.

As a result of the mock review, the unit head and the university administration decided to move the scheduled date of the Board of Examiners visit from late fall 1997, to spring 1998. The advice of the HBCUTSN mock review team proved to be accurate and valuable in the final preparation of the institutional report. The provost assigned a permanent room to house the teacher education program documentation (approximately 900 square feet). Funds were appropriated to furnish this facility and four IBM PCs also were placed in this facility.

Additionally, the field experience coordinator, together with teacher education program faculty and public school teachers, developed a four-phase program to further clarify the early field experience component. Phase 1 now entails classroom observations and affords prospective teachers with the opportunity to observe classrooms and practical applications of theoretical models. Phase 2 involves observation and interaction with K-12 teachers and students in the area in which the candidate plans to teach. Candidates receive incremental exposure to a variety of students in K-12 classrooms. Phase 3 of the prospective teacher's field experience provides opportunities for him/her to apply skills and techniques essential for effective teaching through a practicum experience, providing the candidate with opportunities to develop reflective teaching. Phase 4 entails the senior capstone field experience, student teaching. The field experience refinements were shared with the Teacher Education Council for review and subsequently incorporated into the teacher education program. The field experience phase of the program was reorganized to include a field experience director and an assistant so that all phases of the field experiences are coordinated. A director of the Center for School Change was hired. The director will work collaboratively with state and local schools to provide innovations in the fields of education.

The unit prepared a second institutional report based upon the recommendations of the HBCUTSN mock team's report and submitted the report for review to a second HBCUTSN consultation team. The on-campus mock review was conducted January 10-14, 1998, resulting in additional advice relative to coaching techniques for campus and broader community participants.

Campus and community involvement by unit members continued as Steering Committee members completed the final institutional report. Brown bag luncheons, seminars, a community-wide partnership dinner, and unit presentations to university personnel were held. Posters of the unit's model and theme were posted in all departments of the university as well as in strategic locations across the campus, such as the William C. Jason Library.

The administration, faculty, staff, students, and community have systematically upgraded the university's teacher education program. Specific efforts to improve the program have entailed internal program reviews, seminars and workshops for faculty, staff, students, and external partners, as well as consultations with professional education unit specialists from other institutions and the review of other programs. An NCATE document room was prepared and dedicated for continuous data collection and preparation. Additional staff members were hired to monitor student progress and maintain records.

As a final act in the reweaving for better outcomes, the institutional report was prepared and submitted to the Board of Examiners (BOE) team during the spring of 1998. The BOE team visited the campus on March 21-25, 1998, and conducted the official NCATE campus visitation review. The BOE team indicated that all 20 standards were met.

Reflections by Tommy L. Frederick, Doris E. Wooledge, & Margaret Cole White

When we first began our work as consultants with Delaware State University, we assumed that initial timelines had been implemented to move the teacher education program and the institution toward the goal of achieving national accreditation. We first met the chair of the Education Department and the vice president for academic affairs at the HBCUTSN orientation session in San Francisco in August 1995. Plans were developed to conduct an on-campus needs assessment. From that initial meeting, we learned of the institutional resolve to achieve NCATE accreditation. The needs assessment review was conducted in November 1995 on the institution's campus.

The need to better describe the unit, including its governance structure, and the need to develop a conceptual framework were the two most critical areas of need. Workshops and clinics were suggested as strategies to address the areas of concern. Efforts were made to identify other consultants who could assist the university personnel in addressing the problem areas.

From our analysis, we drew several conclusions. Consistent and persistent leadership appears to be one of the big challenges for the unit at Delaware State University. Consistent leadership had a positive impact on faculty readiness for the process of accreditation.

Another significant challenge for the university faculty was the view that the NCATE process was complex. Would the barriers have diminished if faculty and administrators had been able to view the NCATE process as synonymous with good planning, documenting, and implementing teacher education programs within and among a professional community? The answer is decidedly "yes."

The development of teachers requires teacher scholars who are abreast of best practice, both in the preparation of new teachers and in-service for teachers in the elementary and secondary school settings. Too often, the issue of teacher scholars has not been emphasized at the HBCUs, most likely because of resources. Attention to promoting teachers as scholars, and maintaining intellectual vitality and professional community involvement would add to the teacher education knowledge base and at the same time eradicate the "NCATE mystery."

As Delaware State neared completion of its NCATE review, we noted a new emphasis on building a cohesive knowledge base. The unit appeared to have learned from previous experiences. To address the problem, teams were organized and a retreat was planned. We also observed other lessons learned and amplified in this case; in particular, the Delaware State case shows that

- Faculty development is critical, and the development must be ongoing;
- Systems must be in place for implementing programs and negotiating the NCATE process; and
- Teacher education change is a commitment.

CHAPTER 5

COLLABORATING FOR STABILITY

LeMOYNE-OWEN COLLEGE

Fannye Love
George R. Johnson, Jr.
Andrea Miller

Confronting the Challenge of Change

It has often been said that change is the only constant. Indeed, changes and challenges have been constants from the founding of historically Black colleges and universities more than a century ago to the present. On the eve of a new century, it is both healing and informative for LeMoyne-Owen College in Memphis, Tennessee, to reflect on not only the pains, but also the gains, from our experiences confronting the challenges of change. Over the past decade, LeMoyne-Owen College, like other HBCUs, has been engaged in a struggle for survival. The ups and downs can be likened to a ride on a roller coaster—slow, grinding pulls upward and fast, bumpy pushes downward. We are sharing our ride through the low places as well as the high places in the hope of encouraging others to find new ways of thinking about similar patterns of ups and downs and of providing different means of transforming the downward slopes of pain into the upward pulls toward gains. Our story begins and ends with the upward gains that have had stabilizing effects on the institution. In the middle, we attempt to show how we were able to lift ourselves up from the uneasy, uncertain feelings and actions of the bumpy slopes downward. In all, we have learned valuable lessons from our experiences. We hope our story will make more explicit the implicit understandings that will benefit those who share our long-held commitments to educating teachers for effective work in a pluralistic society.

Institutional Profile

In reflecting on our experiences of preparing for the accreditation of our teacher education program, we saw evidence of both enhancing and inhibiting aspects of change.

Change Enhances Stability. The American Missionary Association founded the institution in 1862 to educate African-Americans. During the 1866 Memphis race riots, the facility was destroyed. In 1870, Dr. Julius LeMoyne donated $20,000 to reopen the school, and one year later it was renamed LeMoyne in his honor. In 1934, LeMoyne College was chartered by the state of Tennessee. In 1954, the S.A. Owen Junior College opened, named in honor of the president of the Tennessee Baptist Missionary and Educational Convention. In 1968, a merger consolidated the two religious and educational organizations, forming the LeMoyne-Owen College that exists today. The school has evolved from institute to high school to junior college to a four-year liberal arts college granting baccalaureate degrees and a master's degree in education. Each of these changes marks significant events in the growth of the college.

LeMoyne-Owen College is a private, four-year, coeducational, liberal arts college, affiliated with the United Church of Christ and the Tennessee Baptist Missionary and Education Convention. It occupies a 15-acre campus about 10 minutes from downtown Memphis and across from the LeMoyne Garden residential area. LeMoyne-Owen College is the only historically African-American college in Memphis. Steeped in heritage, the college has earned a place of distinction among local institutions of higher education, and it is of central importance to the diversification of the teaching workforce in the city of Memphis and the Mid-South. Over the years, approximately 80 percent of the African-American teachers in the Memphis area have been LeMoyne-Owen graduates. Alumni are widely represented in area school systems as teachers, principals, and administrators, including the first African-American superintendent of Memphis City Schools, who is now mayor of the city of Memphis.

Over the years, we have come to view the major institutional changes cited above as having a positive effect on the college. The community looks to the college to help diversify not only its schools, but also its businesses, community organizations, and government offices. Support of the college comes readily from its alumni, faculty, staff, and students, a constant reminder that the college has made historic socioeconomic, cultural, and political contributions to the city and the nation. While this brief accounting of major institutional changes points to some of the positive effects of change on the institution, the enhancements did not come without struggle—without what we have termed the bumpy downward slopes of the roller coaster. Over the past decade, those changes that occurred during the era of preparation for accreditation of the teacher education program provide a glimpse of just how bumpy the ride has been in the recent past, convincing us that change can inhibit stability as well as enhance it.

Change Inhibits Stability. Since its inception, the Division of Education at LeMoyne-Owen College has offered professional education programs. Educating minority teachers has been a major part of the college's service to the community. This service was disrupted in 1983 when the program was discontinued. The Tennessee Department of Education rated the program poorly on the basis of inadequacies in the number of faculty, lack of documentation, and inadequate resources. In addition, our students were not passing the state-mandated basic skills tests at an acceptable level. Because it was clear that these inadequacies could not be addressed without a drastic increase in available resources, the decision was made to discontinue the program. This bumpy ride downward was filled with pain. The end of the program was the beginning of an upward climb, boosted by support from both internal and external constituents.

In 1987-88, a new administration was appointed for the college. New hope came with this appointment, as the new president emphasized the need to continue the college's legacy of training teachers. The teacher education program was revitalized. Federal Title III funds were allocated to assist in the redevelopment of the program. As part of the ride upward, a teacher education unit head was appointed in 1988. In three years, from 1988-89 through 1991-92, the unit was reorganized and programs were submitted to the Tennessee Department of Education. During this process, the Department of Education moved to a new program approval process. The unit then restructured its programs in accordance with new state guidelines.

In 1991, once again, the stability of the program was weakened by the resignation of the president. In about four years, another new president was appointed. The newly appointed president gave strong verbal support to the program and urged the unit to take the next critical steps of becoming a member of the American Association of Colleges for Teacher Education and seeking accreditation by the National Council for Accreditation of Teacher Education. This gave an upward pull toward improved program quality, as most faculty agreed that accreditation should be pursued. The unit head, who had experienced the pain of the unsuccessful 1983 review, cautioned the faculty about the potential lack of readiness for this pursuit. However, in 1992, the unit began the process of developing a conceptual framework and its undergirding knowledge bases and involving the faculty, practicing professionals, students, and administrators. In 1993, the unit applied for membership in AACTE. Three faculty members from the unit attended the AACTE annual meeting that year and met NCATE representatives and two faculty members—potential consultants—from the Sister College Partnership Program at Doane College in Crete, Nebraska. Our spirits were lifted, and the unit decided to seek NCATE accreditation. The unit head invited the state director of teacher education to meet with the faculty of the Divisions of Education and Arts and Sciences, enabling us to ask questions and gather information about the process.

There were many slopes and peaks during the period. The unit head, who had guided the program toward many successes from 1988 to 1994, resigned. In 1994-95, the president appointed a full-time faculty member as acting unit head. This appointee had extensive knowledge of the state certification standards and an understanding of the people and the culture of LeMoyne-Owen College. She also had prior experiences with the Southern Association of Colleges and Schools' (SACS) accreditation process. She continued efforts to build a community among the teacher education faculty, develop a systematic filing system for students' records, and clarify the conceptual framework as it emerged from faculty discussions. The NCATE preconditions report was submitted and approved in 1994.

In June 1995, the acting chair and a recently hired faculty member resigned. The downward slopes of instability continued with a seemingly endless cycle of resignations and new appointments. In 1995-96, an interim unit head was appointed, but the coordinator of special projects and a faculty member had resigned. Another faculty member stepped down from full- to part-time work in the department. By the summer of 1995, the third president since 1987 had resigned, leaving the college to be governed by a three-person committee. To further exacerbate the situation, the fourth unit head since 1987 resigned in 1996. We were in the midst of a downward slope, felt not only from the top but also from the bottom. This pattern of simultaneous top-down and bottom-up changes makes accreditation a mission impossible, the proof of which is that we pushed onward, if not upward, toward an NCATE accreditation visit. And, no, we did not fare well in the review, but, yes, we now have a new president and are in the process of pushing upward toward stability. We have learned much from the damaged spirits of this roller-coaster excursion, which is reflected in the responses to change, as well as the program elements that sustained us, which are described below as stabilizing forces.

"No pain, no gain" is a statement often used as a testament to hard work leading to a goal. Responses to the discomforts of change vary, but all point to aspects of the damaged spirit that must be healed in order for the accreditation process to move forward.

Administrators Reassess Roles, Governance, and Knowledge

Preparation for accreditation presents a special challenge to administrators. In our case, one of the greatest challenges for the vice president for academic affairs (VPAA) was defining the appropriate role in the accreditation process for persons operating in the higher levels of administration. Shared governance, we discovered, is a second necessary element of success in the accreditation process, not only because of the need to show this pattern to external evaluators, but most particularly because of the rapid changes in administration at our college. And third, knowledge of the requirements of accrediting agencies makes the most convincing case that support mechanisms were needed within the administration. From the perspective of higher-level administrators, the importance of this triad of roles, governance, and knowledge is revealed.

By 1994, administrators at the top level of the system began to realize that serious action must be taken, as we were faced not only with NCATE accreditation, but also with accreditation by SACS, the regional college accreditation board. In 1994, the unit head (1988-94) and the VPAA had to assess, evaluate, and build the new graduate program. The program was to be evaluated by SACS within the year, and there was a possibility that it would be removed from candidacy for accreditation. The governance structure caused a problem. The graduate program had a dean who reported to the president, not the unit head or the VPAA. Given the leadership style of the supervisor and given the absence of adequate staffing of the unit, the VPAA began to focus less on NCATE accreditation and more on the SACS accreditation.

More important, concerns were heightened by the realization that those directly responsible for providing leadership—the unit head, the VPAA, and the president—were managing by crisis. There was direct communication between the president and the unit head. There was direct communication between the unit head and the VPAA. But at no point did the three sit down to develop a strategic plan for future action. The critical point here is that the primary leaders were not necessarily on the same page with regard to, if when, and how the preparation for NCATE should proceed. The planning process was missing, creating confusion about the role of the VPAA in the NCATE process and leaving the SACS process as the highest priority.

Clearly, the force that drives crisis management is crisis—in this case, a series of crises. Planning often takes a back seat to management when resources are limited and long-term decisions must be made in a short time.

A combination of crisis management, unstable governance procedures, and inadequate resources prompted the resignation in 1994 of the capable unit head, who had been in this role since 1988. This resignation occurred before the SACS accreditation visit, and all plans for NCATE accreditation halted. The 1994-95 interim unit head was appointed from the ranks of the faculty. The VPAA was then left with the responsibility of acting as the head of the unit's graduate program and pushing the unit forward with NCATE. The VPAA had to learn about the NCATE accreditation process, thoroughly and quickly. With this quick study came a better understanding of the past failures of support, the needs of the unit, and the ways to assist in securing the consultative services and other support systems needed. As the quick study turned into a critical, labor-intensive process, it began to bear fruit. The new insights gained were of tremendous value in clarifying the role of upper administrators, in articulating the needs of the institution, and in appreciating the challenges the unit faced and the ways of confronting them.

More time would have been a welcome commodity. However, we had neither the time for further delays nor the resources for preparation at the desired level. The review went forth, and we have now begun anew with a commitment to build on our strengths. One of those strengths is the assistance we received through the HBCU Technical Support Network. Another is the partnership programs that have continued their development through the bumpy slopes of the challenges of change.

Stabilizing Forces

As we reflect on our experiences, the question that has resurfaced time and time again is what were the stabilizing factors. Two of the more obvious ones are the consistent support received from the HBCU Network and the continued thrust toward building partnerships.

The Network Becomes a Staple. In 1992-93, a two-day spring retreat was held. An external consultant worked with the faculty on the NCATE process and overview of the standards. The unit faculty identified key aspects of the program, concepts/knowledge, and ways to conceptualize the knowledge base. By the end of the 1994-95 academic year, the acting chair and a faculty member had attended an informational meeting of the HBCU Network, and the Network had assigned three consultants to work with LeMoyne-Owen College. One of the consultants was from Doane College, an institution with which we had a partnership, and this provided some continuity and consistency with our prior work. Over time, we were involved in three phases of the Network training model: assessment, education, and coaching.

The HBCU Network consultants conducted a needs assessment visit in January 1995. We were commended for our commitment to providing quality minority teachers, serving nontraditional students, and revitalizing the program. We also received valuable feedback on ways to strengthen the program, with suggestions ranging from governance to documentation. Immediately apparent were the discrepancies between our self-evaluations and the team's evaluations. The challenge here was to enable us to see ourselves as others see us. The needs assessment was especially useful in redirecting our attention to the need to fine-tune some aspects of the conceptual framework, clarify the governance structure, generate new resources, and examine our ways of documenting our actions. This phase was the beginning of a relationship that provided some continuity and encouragement for continuing to move toward improving the quality of our program.

The HBCU Network met in San Francisco in August 1995, and the interim unit head and the two Network consultants scheduled a consulting visit to LeMoyne-Owen College for September. Recall that during the summer of 1995 the college's president resigned. For the 1995-96 academic year, the college was governed by a three-person committee. At the September meeting, the governing committee chair met with the Network consultants and assured them of the institution's commitment to this process. Professional clinics were conducted, the conceptual framework was reviewed, and an activity timeline was established based on the results of the needs assessment. In an assessment of our progress, the team noted faculty enthusiasm and assurances of support by our three-member governing board as signs of well-being. Again, we were encouraged, for again we felt as though we were moving in a structured manner toward greater stability.

A second educative phase clinic was held in January 1996. The interim unit head had prepared a draft of the conceptual framework to be reviewed during this clinic. This framework reflected the direction of the interim unit head while retaining elements of the previous drafts. The promised computers and other equipment had not materialized. This was a difficult time for the unit head, because some faculty members were unable to embrace some of the elements of the framework. Through the clinics, faculty were able to resolve differences and finalize major decisions about the framework. It became increasingly clear to the unit head that a vast amount of work remained to be done. The questions that were raised this late in the process signaled trouble:

Where do we start in getting ready for NCATE vs. the state review? How will other divisions be organized for developing their course syllabi according to our conceptual framework? How does the Department of Health Education, Wellness, and Fitness fit into this scheme? Is there an NCATE resource room in this division?

It was easy to ignore the trouble signals, because the participants were indeed diverse, consisting of faculty from education and arts and sciences, adjunct faculty, students, principals, and assessment personnel. In this diverse group were some who had not been actively involved previously. Besides, we were very hopeful that a new president would be on board in time for the coaching phase of the training, which was scheduled for July, only three months before the official visit.

Hope began to fade as the July coaching phase came to an end. This coaching, characterized by a mock accreditation visit, indicated that much work still remained to be done. In the meantime, two faculty members accepted positions at other institutions for fall 1996. It was not possible to replace them in time for the NCATE visit. By the time of the visit, faculty were at an all-time low, but managed to get through the visit. We had to count getting through as a success, given our bumpy roads and jerky pulls downward. Two months after the NCATE/state visit, the unit head resigned. By the following January (1997), we noted signs of resilience. The president had begun to talk the talk that we had so long sought.

Partnerships Yield Unexpected Benefits. The other sustaining force in our roller coaster excursion is our partnership programs, which continued to grow. In 1992-93, the unit faculty met with the president and the VPAA to discuss collaboration with Doane College. The discussion also included the schedule of the first visit to Doane. In January 1993, three faculty members and 30 students from Doane College visited the campus and Memphis City Schools to fulfill the NCATE requirements involving diversity and multicultural perspectives in field experiences.

Four unit faculty members and 15 students traveled to Doane College; participated in education classes, open discussion, and tours of the campus; and visited schools in Crete and Lincoln, Nebraska.

Two Doane College members of the NCATE Board of Examiners facilitated a weekend workshop for the unit faculty in 1994. These consultants' prior visit had provided them with a sense of context and established initial relationships between the consultants and faculty. As a result of the workshop, the LeMoyne-Owen College faculty were prepared to complete the preconditions documents and to identify tasks for program development related to the NCATE standards. The faculty and consultants drafted a timeline for an NCATE on-site visit in the fall of 1994 and an accompanying budget.

The collaborative exchange continued with a second reciprocal visit of LeMoyne-Owen students and staff to Doane College in April. The visit included meetings with recruiters from the Omaha and Lincoln public schools and a breakfast served by the Lincoln chapter of the National Council of Negro Women. Three Doane faculty and students had visited LeMoyne-Owen in January 1994.

This cooperative program existed despite unstable surroundings. Both institutions benefited, for each was able to realize its goals of greater diversity. Our students and faculty gained from the experience of working in collaborative learning groups and observing and participating in integrated instruction, assertive discipline, and technology labs—all in a rural, predominantly White environment. In turn, the Doane students and faculty benefited from observing and participating in school settings that were predominantly African-American and urban. Students were required to keep journals. One student from Doane College wrote:

My first cultural encounter was a very emotional and powerful one at the National Civil Rights Museum home of Lorraine Motel where Martin Luther King Jr. was killed. As I watched a film in the museum, an African-American woman and her daughter stood next to me and watched also.... I looked over at the woman next to me, not really knowing why and I saw a tear roll down her cheek. She then looked at me and I looked at her. Silence. Then her daughter accidentally ran into my purse, which held my camera and I reached down to her daughter and said, "I'm sorry." I meant I was sorry for her head bumping into my camera and for the pain white people have caused African-Americans. The little girl's mother looked at me, wiped her tear, gave me a look like she knew I was sorry, not really a smile, but not a frown either, and then they left. I really do not understand how she feels. But I am trying to.

Beyond the benefit of the Memphis culture, other students wrote about the benefits of their exposure to the urban school environment:

The most important thing that has happened during this term for me is that it has opened my mind towards other human beings and their differences. I have never really thought of myself as being biased towards a certain culture, but as I look back at all things that may have happened to me or that I may have said, I can see now that I was. Usually I consider myself to be a pretty tolerant person and it was a real eye-opener for me to realize that in certain aspects, I wasn't.

In her project report, the consultant of Doane College wrote:

> The student exchanges to Memphis and Nebraska provide students from each campus with study and experiences about appropriate strategies for individual learning needs, especially for students culturally diverse by race and rural/urban experiences.

Our partnership was highlighted in the HBCU Network newsletter, another encouraging activity. We began to see the partnerships, this and others, as our signature piece, one that provided an opportunity to be creative in translating the diversity standards of NCATE into real programs.

On November 15, 1995, a small group of faculty from the Division of Education and Graduate Studies, an executive from Cummins Engine Foundation, and a school superintendent from the Bartholomew Consolidated School Corporation (both in Columbus, Indiana) met for the entire day and discussed the possibility of a partnership between a historically Black college, a predominantly White school district, and a Fortune 500 company (Cummins Engine). We decided to have a practicum experience wherein students from LeMoyne-Owen College would travel to Columbus and student-teach in the Bartholomew Consolidated School Corporation. The plan was jointly developed with specific responsibilities for students—for example, to act as a resource and active participant in the classroom and be a learner in the host's home, while also talking openly and respectfully with mentors (supervising teachers), principals, and host families about the differences between Memphis and Columbus. The eight LeMoyne-Owen students, who were selected from a group of 30, spent three weeks observing and working in the Columbus schools. These students were featured at the college's annual education symposium, "Effective Pedagogy for Urban Learners." Several teachers from the Columbus school district also participated in the symposium, creating a rich exchange of information on diversity.

Two other partnerships evolved within the city of Memphis. The Dewitt Wallace-Reader's Digest Fellows program is jointly sponsored by LeMoyne-Owen and the University of Memphis. Its goal is to develop pathways by which students are trained to become effective teachers in urban schools that serve multicultural populations. LeMoyne-Owen and the University of Memphis have a common advisory board that meets regularly to monitor the progress of the program. Project Teach is a collaborative effort of LeMoyne-Owen College, the University of Memphis, Shelby State Community College, and the Memphis City Schools. Project Teach selects its participants from a pool of minority educational assistants employed by the Memphis City Schools. These educational assistants may have worked in the schools for years, and some have bachelor's degrees, but they are not licensed to teach. Project Teach provides training that leads to certification. The Memphis Center for Urban Partnership is still another local collaborative, involving LeMoyne-Owen College, Shelby State Community College, the University of Memphis, the Memphis City Schools, and the Schering-Plough Corporation. This program uses a team approach to solving systemic problems pertaining to retention of students and graduation from secondary and postsecondary educational institutions.

During the times when internal resources were hard to obtain, we were able to keep ourselves moving upward by further developing our externally supported partnership programs. And this represents one of the ways that the partnerships proved to be of immense value to us. Second, these partnerships are a means for HBCUs to ensure diverse clinical settings for their students, despite the difficulty that many experience with full-time enrollment of non-African-American students. Similarly, predominantly White institutions value the partnerships as a way to enhance their diversity efforts.

Lessons Learned: Hold Fast to Principles of Change and Growth

Lesson 1. A successful NCATE accreditation review requires stability from top to bottom and from bottom to top. Our experiences suggest that accreditation is a mission impossible when there are instabilities at both ends of the institutional structure. With each shift, we felt that we were starting the process anew. We now recognize this as a building process that takes consistency in administrative style, resource allocations, and division of labor over a long period of time.

Lesson 2. Having one person wear too many hats can cause more problems than it solves. Seeking NCATE/state approval is a difficult task for small, private HBCUs. We had difficulty with financial stability, professional vitality, and governance procedures—all conditions that cause faculty members to wear too many hats. LeMoyne-Owen was a financially struggling institution at the time of the NCATE/state preparation and review. Because the state of Tennessee is an NCATE partnership state, two teams were on campus. While it was apparent that all of us were dedicated to the cause, it also was apparent that we were insufficiently staffed to carry out the multiple tasks that had been initiated.

Lesson 3. Hard work, good intentions, and dedication are not always enough. The unit faculty and the consultants worked long hours preparing for this visit, because there were only eight weeks between the mock assessment visit and the actual visit. The chairperson for the NCATE team resigned before the visit. Unit faculty members were not able to get the institutional report to him in a timely manner. Another chair was selected by NCATE, but this chairperson's university was being visited by NCATE two weeks before the LeMoyne-Owens visit. Through it all, the unit faculty members received recognition of overall strengths from the state of Tennessee team members for 1) clearly recognizing that the training of teacher candidates is an institution-wide responsibility, and 2) having a caring faculty who made themselves easily accessible to students.

Lesson 4. Recognizing your strengths and building on them will yield rich dividends. Our strengths came from the technical support and partnerships, which were supported by external funds and by external personnel. Perhaps these times of working with outsiders were our greatest sources of energy. Certainly the validations of positive aspects of our students, our program, and our efforts helped to smooth some of the bumpy slopes of the roller coaster excursions.

In conclusion, to be successful with this process, the unit must have sufficient support—financial resources, faculty, and clerical staff—as well as teaching loads that allow faculty members to grow intellectually. It is important to be able to meet regularly to discuss issues, needs, and concerns of the unit faculty and students. Documentation is a weakness that we are addressing, because much of what we had accomplished could not be demonstrated in a convincing manner. Finally, the administration must be involved and understand the process from beginning to end. As we begin again, the higher-level administration has moved toward a greater understanding of the process.

Postscript from the President of LeMoyne-Owen College

George Robert Johnson Jr., Esq.

As one who entered the college in 1996, I have grown from the wisdom of the practices that preceded my presidency. From rapid encounters with the challenges to reflective critical analysis of the potential solutions, we see the importance of leadership from the top. Certainly no area contributed more to this understanding than that of the Department of Education. There is, then, a message in this experience that is of importance to share with other presidents who may not as yet have translated the concept of "buy-in from the top" into actions most needed to facilitate the accreditation process for teacher education programs. Among the most critical areas for consideration by presidents are infrastructure development; commitment and understanding at the higher levels of administration; and the utilization of strong collaboratives with schools, other higher education institutions, the corporate sector, and the community.

Infrastructure development begins and ends with financial stability. At LeMoyne-Owen College, we began with a capital campaign and ended with the commitment to make our supporters proud of their assistance. In operational terms, we have to ensure that both the leaders and the academic teams were strong, and this has meant the hiring of new administrators, including a vice president for academic affairs and a chair of the Division of Education, as well as the hiring of new faculty members in the division. In part, the critical analysis of needs helped inform the search for persons who could best fit the immediate and long-term needs of the Division of Education. We are now stronger from both the top to the bottom and the bottom to the top.

Special steps have been taken to ensure that the flow of top-down and bottom-up inputs receives the attention that leads to understanding and commitment. This is an on-going process, which we are initiating through faculty-administrator retreats. With the Division of Education, detailed information will be provided to ensure that the entire community understands and appreciates the roles, expectations, and any further responsibilities.

We have discovered that collaboratives warrant the attention of the highest levels of administration, for they can be used to address two issues that are likely to come to the attention of the president: financial resources and diversity. While the education program must have solid financial support, the collaboratives can greatly enhance areas of enrichment that are not normally part of the base budget. Regarding diversity, it is clear that HBCUs, and especially private ones, face the special challenge of attracting scholarships and other means of financial support for nonminority students. It becomes important for us to work toward identifying nontraditional but effective ways of realizing the values of diversity and meeting the diversity standards of accreditation bodies. I am now convinced that through collaboratives it should be possible to achieve results and to meet diversity standards that are found in accreditation guidelines. Although we have not yet worked out the solutions, we have asked the question of how to use collaboratives to better achieve the benefits of diversity.

From a presidential perspective, I strongly suggest that the three areas discussed here—infrastructure, commitment, and collaboratives—warrant early and persistent attention, not only from the bottom up but also from the top down.

Reflections by

Gwendolyn Trotter

Several years ago the U.S. Department of Education (OERI, 1993) disseminated a monograph, *School Change: Models and Process.* This monograph described change with three metaphors "fix the administration, fix the faculty, or fix the system." This metaphorical triad seems pertinent to the LeMoyne-Owen case. The prevailing theme is that of fixing the administration and the impact of the president on teacher education change and accreditation. The "fix the faculty" was not a theme because another prevailing theme was that there were no faculty to fix. The concept of fixing the system was a theme, but as one read the case, it became clear that the system consisted of multiple fragments and a hodgepodge of many subsystems. These subsystems appeared to be politically and culturally unique to LeMoyne-Owen. One even gets a glimpse of the "Golden Age Mythology" which is a view of back when things were great.

It appears that LeMoyne-Owen has been in a constant state of crisis as related to teacher education change and the accreditation process. There also is a "polemical view" that we can't we don't have we need we're not ready, etc. This view is probably accurate, but one wonders if the unit has considered "evolutionary change" which is based upon examined experiences. As one continues through the case, it appears that the unit has not been able to pull together a professional community that can examine where they've been and where they need to go. Experiences are tied intricately to the deeply rooted historical context thus letting go appears to be a major challenge for this unit. The crisis mode is exacerbated by lack of staff cohesion and stability. Leadership is obviously a problem for the unit, but one wonders, can a unit negotiate the accrediting process regardless of leadership if a professional community exists with commitment? At the same time, one must readily accept that this unit had major resource problems that would impact professional community as well as the leadership's attempt to force the accrediting process.

There are several lessons that teacher education units can learn by studying LeMoyne-Owen's challenges as they pursued accreditation. First, minimal human and physical resources must be in place. It is apparent that LeMoyne-Owen did not have adequate resources in place to negotiate the process. However, also note in other cases, teacher education programs with meager resources were able to utilize the professional community and family concept to overcome the resource issue. Second, it appeared that LeMoyne-Owen was handicapped by the historical and cultural "habits of action and mind." These "habits of action and mind" appear to come from years of instability and "absence of critical mass of faculty/staff" without the history. In other words, having the history doesn't always help the unit. This history served as a deterrent to progress. Third, faculty must be empowered or empower themselves to make changes. Changes should be evolutionary (developmental). Regardless of resources, empowerment is critical. It is not sufficient to say "we can't change because we don't have resources."

It isn't sufficient to say "we can't change because of the administration." Fourth, personalizing and examining experiences from a "what happened to me" viewpoint creates hurdles that trip not only "the personalizer" but the unit as well. Experiences need to be examined but within the context of shared experiences and the goal of using these experiences for continuous progress and improvement.

CHAPTER 6

A TRIP BECOMES A JOURNEY

VIRGINIA UNION UNIVERSITY

Glennie Mueller
Donna Jones Miles
Delores R. Greene

When Virginia Union University (VUU) was founded in 1865 in Richmond, its mission was the education of newly emancipated slaves. As it evolved, the cornerstone of the university's conceptual foundation was theological training and the preparation of leaders and teachers of generations to come. VUU's urban setting has made it possible for this private, coed, historically Black institution to serve Richmond's nearly 200,000 residents and to enable students from diverse backgrounds to fulfill their academic goals.

For more than 132 years, the dedicated faculty and staff of Virginia Union University have prepared some of the nation's leading scholars, religious leaders, business leaders, and politicians, including L. Douglas Wilder, a former Governor of Virginia, and Walter E. Fauntroy, a former Delegate to the U.S. House of Representatives from the District of Columbia. In this nurturing, yet demanding and scholarly, environment, students have every opportunity to succeed. What makes success possible is the notion of family that undergirds day-to-day life at the university. Faculty and staff throughout the campus are known for the personal rapport they develop with students and the encouragement they offer. Their knowledge of students' individual academic goals allows for personal counseling. Campus becomes like a home away from home. Letters and testimonials from Virginia Union graduates speak fondly of the family atmosphere that was such an integral part of their academic journey and that helped sustain them in their chosen careers.

The university's family atmosphere has also been a hallmark of the College of Liberal Arts & Sciences, which comprises two schools—Arts & Sciences and the Sydney Lewis School of Business Administration—and confers bachelor of arts and bachelor of science degrees. The Graduate School of Theology offers Master of Divinity and Doctor of Ministry degrees.

Virginia Union strives to compete with institutions of similar size and scope while remaining true to its mission and goals. It does so through a combination of administrative and faculty development, student and staff involvement in the decision-making process, curriculum evaluation and development, strategic planning, and alumni and parent cooperation.

Forging a Program, Molding Future Teachers

Teacher education is the second largest of VUU's 11 undergraduate academic units. Serving more than 150 students pursuing teaching careers, the department abounds with activity and energy. The result: a reputation for excellence in teacher education and preparation that is known statewide. Each year, 20 to 30 new teachers graduate from the program, and more than 90 percent of them either accept teaching posts nationally and locally or enter graduate school.

There had been no formal department of education at Virginia Union until 1955, when the college established four divisions—humanities, social sciences, mathematics, and education and psychology. An education faculty member in the 1950s might teach philosophy, history, elementary curriculum, and elementary school science, and also supervise student teachers. Teacher preparation programs and related teacher education activities comprised the new Division of Education and Psychology, which offered programs to prepare elementary school teachers. An associate major in secondary education was paired with the content area major.

Students were required to have not only two years or at least 48 credit hours in the liberal arts, but also content and pedagogical courses mandated by the Virginia Department of Education. Graduates received a Collegiate Professional Certificate from the Commonwealth of Virginia.

In 1967, VUU created the Department of Elementary and Secondary Education and required that secondary education students be admitted to the Division of Education and Psychology. Selected students did their student teaching under supervisors outside of Virginia, while the majority interned locally. Eventually a child development center and curriculum library were added as an educational laboratory for pre-service teachers. In 1969, VUU's Education Department was accredited by the Southern Association of Schools and Colleges.

In 1987, the Virginia Board of Education restructured teacher education programs according to recommendations made in a report by the Commission on Excellence in Education. The guidelines abolished the undergraduate degree in teacher education, capped at 18 the number of semester hours required for professional education courses, and required students to earn a degree in an arts and sciences discipline.

Until 1989, the Division of Education and Psychology had primary responsibility for preparing students to teach. Undergraduate programs were offered in early education, middle education, secondary education, and special education.

From 1989 until 1993, VUU's education program was in transition. The essential design of the restructured programs had been developed by a former VUU chair who left the institution unexpectedly. Other significant participants in the design of the new program, which had been approved in 1989, also were unavailable. Numerous factors, including personnel changes, delayed a smooth transition into the new program requirements:

— In academic year 1988-1989, a new chair of the Division of Education and Psychology and a new chair of the Department of Teacher Education provided leadership.

— A university reorganization made Education and Psychology a separate division during the 1989-1990 academic year. The chair of the Department of Teacher Education left the university. A new chair provided leadership and reported to the chairman of the Division of Humanities.

— During the 1990-1991 academic year, the chair of the Department of Education resigned and an acting chair was appointed to complete the academic year. The acting chair remained through the next academic year, but missed significant time because of illness.

— The Department of Teacher Education became the Teacher Preparation Program and the chair became the coordinator of Education Programs for the 1992-1993 academic year, reporting to a new chair for the Division of Humanities.

A phase-in period was initiated for the restructured program, but students graduating after July 1990 were expected to meet the new program standards. Personnel changes, university reorganization, change of program status, and multiple leadership shifts had significantly affected teacher education.

The program had met state requirements, but many of the faculty failed to capture the vision or to fully comprehend changes taking place. As a result, much time was spent educating new department heads and faculty. While the restructured program was designed primarily by a small committee, the broad collaboration needed for its effective and efficient implementation was absent. The university's collective vision for teacher education was clouded, and full implementation of the restructured program was hampered by continuous delays.

The state's mandated changes in the curriculum meant that students who enrolled after July 1, 1990, could no longer major in elementary, middle school, or secondary education; they had to major in specific subject areas such as mathematics or English. Also, as a result of the changes, students were limited to 18 course hours in pedagogy, down from as many as 30 hours previously allowed.

The restructured Teacher Education Plan called for licensure areas in early-middle education (K-8) with an English Language Arts major and in secondary education (9-12) with a major in English, French, mathematics, biology, chemistry, history/political science, psychology, or business information systems. Students also majored in instrumental and vocal/choral music (K-12) and in special education—mental retardation (K-12).

Faculty also were greatly affected by the new state requirements. They were challenged to develop a creative approach to the curriculum that included as many practical courses as possible. Both students and faculty members had to adjust to differences in programs while complying with the new requirements.

But the change and stability the program needed were realized in 1993 with the hiring of a new director who had impressive credentials and the respect of the academic and professional community. It was not long before her skillful leadership resulted in a deliberate and systematic renewal and revision of the pre-service teacher education component. Policies and procedures were gradually initiated to enhance day-to-day operations and develop and achieve long-range goals.

From the Fire to the Fishbowl

It was not long, however, before the programmatic and personnel changes that were underway were derailed. On a frigid January evening in 1994, fire swept through Martin E. Gray Hall, the stately granite building that had housed the university's Teacher Education Program since its inception in 1923. The blaze—touched off by an arsonist or by faulty wiring—burned well into the winter night. Throngs of faculty members, students, and neighbors huddled together in stunned amazement as the fire in Gray Hall raged. Gone were alumni records, national exams, student scores, computers, personal collections of children's literature, tools of the profession—all melted into charred mounds or reduced to ashes.

The next morning Gray Hall was shrouded under a veil of dingy ice and soot, accented by a sense of quiet and calm. Whispered voices occasionally punctured the frigid morning air. There were compassionate hugs, heads that wagged and shook in disbelief, and plenty of tears. There also was a determination to pick up the pieces and forge ahead.

Alumnus Quentin Hicks, class of 1996, credits the Gray Hall fire for his academic turnaround. In a recent letter to his former professors in the Teacher Education program, he recalled his less-than-stellar academic start. He had come to VUU with lofty goals and ambition, he said, but his performance and work had been "mediocre."

The fire, Hicks recalled, was the spark he needed to help capture his dream of becoming a teacher. "I watched Martin E. Gray Hall burn to the ground. When I went to bed that night, I realized that if I didn't get my priorities straight that my life and career as a teacher would also burn to the ground. In the process [of personal change] I pleased my parents, my teachers, myself, and my God." Hicks, who is now in his second year of teaching in the Chesapeake Public School System, graduated from VUU with a 3.0 grade point average.

In the days that followed the fire, what remained of the Teacher Education Program was relocated to a leased building across the street from the main campus and a few feet from a busy intersection. Hence, makeshift classroom space was bombarded by the noise of vehicular traffic.

The complete work area for Teacher Education became a glassed-in space surrounded by administrative offices. The one room the program occupied was tucked away in the corner of the building, encased in two walls of storefront glass.

The Teacher Education Program survived in a "fishbowl" for the next 20 months. Students prepared decorative cardboard boxes as partitions designating office space for the program director. While a methods class was conducted in the front of the room, other faculty and staff counseled students in the back.

The fire presented many obstacles for the program, but it also offered an opportunity to redirect the future of teacher education at Virginia

Union. The program's new director began refocusing not only on new policies and procedures that would shape the future of teacher education, but on achieving excellence in the profession. From the ashes came the determination faculty and administrators needed to advance the program, to make it competitive, and to rethink traditional approaches to teacher preparation. The Teacher Education Program intended to do more than just replace its curriculum or a few textbooks and equipment. Instead, its growth and rebirth were designed to be slow, methodical, and deliberate.

The 98-year-old Martin Gray Hall reopened in 1996, two years after it went up in flames. Today, the transformation that has taken place inside the historic structure is as amazing as what took place on the outside. Much thought and research went into the redesign of the physical facility and the acquisition of new equipment and materials. Administrative staff worked with Teacher Education faculty to meet many of VUU's initiatives and goals.

Also, as part of the transformation and restoration process, the curriculum was analyzed in terms of new standards and best practices. Faculty members traveled to surrounding colleges and universities of similar size and goals and public school and community experts came to Virginia Union to share ideas and to make recommendations for moving the program forward.

**National Accreditation: A Springboard
to the Future**

In 1995, just one year after the fire, the program

applied for and received a grant from NCATE to pursue national accreditation through the HBCU Technical Support Network. The quest for national accreditation was just the springboard the program needed to propel it forward into the 21st century.

Many on campus thought that a faculty of three (with one full-time staff person), operating out of temporary quarters on a shoestring budget, was phenomenal. But the timing could not have been better for embarking on such a mission. The Virginia Department of Education had not reviewed the university's Teacher Education Program since it was restructured in 1989.

The program may have been short on staff and resources, but the vital ingredient needed to make national accreditation a reality existed. Systematic, structured, reflective practice guided the faculty's interaction with students, staff, and administrators. High standards that the faculty had adopted for itself and for its students were constantly under review. On a small, private, liberal arts campus like Virginia Union, building good faculty-student rapport can make the difference between student success and failure. Achieving those elements can be time-consuming, but they are necessary if a professional unit is to be maintained. Administrative support and open communication with major field and general studies faculty also are necessary. These were among ingredients already in place in the program.

Through national accreditation, faculty and administrators were determined to find a way to give students a program with credibility that could not be diminished by external forces. Pursuing national accreditation has provided the opportunity to expand Virginia Union's Teacher Education Program and recruit the best and brightest students.

Following notification of acceptance in the NCATE/AACTE Network, two members of the program faculty attended the initial orientation in San Francisco. The full-time faculty of three, and the one full-time staff person, turned immediately to the needs assessment instrument and the preconditions report which would identify program areas that needed improvement. With the help of the Teacher Education Council, the unit submitted the preconditions report in December 1995, and preparation for the needs assessment visit became the next phase of the process. This phase proved to be a rich learning experience that has given the program's faculty the opportunity to survey teacher education at Virginia Union through the eyes of outside professionals. Faculty, staff, and administrators were buoyed by the positive feedback from program graduates interviewed independently by accreditation officials as part of the formal process.

The results of the needs assessment process, specifically the areas designated for improvement, were often in line with assessments made in-house. But it was not until these findings were reported by the Network consultant team that teacher education administrators realized what the staff and faculty had been saying all along about the program areas that needed improvement. Under NCATE scrutiny, the strengths and weaknesses of the Teacher

Education Program were laid bare. The process highlighted several areas for further work.

The unit's response to the needs assessment report regarding **development of the conceptual framework** was to form a Conceptual Framework Focus Group from members of the Teacher Education Council—university staff, faculty, and candidates—who met for brainstorming sessions, followed by research and writing. Data from a two-day workshop conducted by the unit's lead consultant, along with a consultant with additional expertise, provided much of the material for the content. Drafts were distributed to council members, the university community, and public school personnel for their feedback. The knowledge base references, the visual image, and the components of the framework were a result of input from many sources. The final product was then disseminated to the university and professional community. The conceptual framework and its components are continually monitored to maintain consistency with current research and best practice.

The need to include **multicultural and diversity initiatives** in the curriculum also was addressed. An initial step was the writing of a grant proposal to conduct a diversity workshop during the summer. The grant was awarded and a two-week workshop was held, led by experts in diversity issues and attended by both Virginia Union faculty and faculty from area colleges and universities. The increased inclusion of multicultural and diversity activities in course syllabi and the assignment of candidates to more diverse field-based sites were also implemented. Previous collaboration with an area college having a predominantly White population was renewed. The inclusion of multicultural and diversity sessions in American Education Week programs became an annual event. A formal diversity plan was developed that provided a format for continued inclusion and awareness of such issues in the unit.

In response to the needs assessment report, **technology** initiatives already in existence were organized into a formal technology plan. This plan consisted of three levels that reflected both immediate and long-range goals. The computer laboratory in teacher education had begun as part of a federally funded Title III grant in the late 1980s. The fire had completely destroyed the computer resources. New equipment upgraded the lost resources. By the time the needs assessment occurred, it was again time to upgrade the existing technology. The data in the technology plan helped to prepare for these additions.

A university-wide Technology Committee was formed; it included individuals from area public schools and colleges as well as the unit faculty member charged with monitoring technology. A technology seminar was planned for the summer that was funded by a grant received by the unit. Participants included Teacher Education Council members. Leaders for the seminar were unit faculty, Virginia Department of Education and public school personnel, and area community college faculty.

Field-based experiences were expanded in response to the needs assessment report. A major emphasis was to include more diverse settings for candidates to experience other cultures and diverse environments. It also was clear that the field-based program should reflect the conceptual framework. The developmental model for clinical and field experiences that had been in place in the unit was revised to coincide with components and outcomes of the conceptual framework.

The department also addressed some areas of improvement identified in the team's needs assessment feedback report by participating in professional conferences, collaborating with discipline-based faculty, developing the Department of Teacher Education and Interdisciplinary Studies, restructuring the Teacher Education Council, and designating the department as the unit.

As an added, and perhaps unexpected, benefit of the needs assessment process, the university was prompted to articulate its level of commitment to teacher education. VUU faculty, alumni, students, and administrators have a vested interest in accreditation. They share the vision.

Regular workshops and conferences continue to provide opportunities for learning and insight into the process of acquiring excellence through national accreditation. Each department is examining its own program for areas of improvement and efficiency. Other university departments also are reflecting on their role in the accreditation process—curriculum and collaboration.

The first Network team visit was delayed because of a snow and ice storm. When the four-member team finally arrived on campus, the meeting went smoothly and was productive for all who attended.

The exit interview with the Network team and the feedback they offered were constructive. They concluded that although the unit had shown proof of readiness to continue pursuit of NCATE accreditation, significant challenges still had to be overcome.

In the educative phase of the process, the faculty participated in a workshop that focused on redesigning the governance structure. The restoration of departmental status for teacher education became a reality in July 1996. The workshop also focused on the development of proper documentation of meetings and student advising.

As the unit continued to move through the educative and collaborative phases of the accreditation process, the education faculty remained a cohesive body focused on the goal of accreditation. The university faculty became more vested in contributing to the success of the project. A vital ingredient that kept everyone at Virginia Union moving ahead was the commitment and support of a forward-thinking administration that has embraced and clearly articulated the goal of national accreditation.

Reflections by

JoAnne S. Drane and Gwendolyn Trotter

The Network's formal involvement with the Teacher Education Program at Virginia Union

University occurred two years after the devastating fire that physically destroyed the entire program: building, equipment, materials, supplies, files, plans, and, momentarily, the hopes and dreams of its faculty and students. Before the fire, the leadership of the program had changed every year for three years. While it took quite a while for the physical destruction to be repaired, hopes and dreams for the program's new beginning took wing quickly. The challenge envisioned for teacher education at VUU appeared to be "why not use this disaster as an opportunity for excellence?" Later, in the thinking and rebuilding process, national accreditation became a part of the vision.

As indicated earlier, the major areas identified through needs assessment and consultation for program attention and development were governance, collaboration, design, and infusion of the conceptual framework and technology. These areas have been addressed by administrative actions and through clinics or workshops, committee meetings, long-range planning, and other activities. Teacher education has been elevated to departmental status, and special education licensure, which previously operated outside the unit, is now housed administratively within the unit. The Teacher Education Council has been reorganized and restructured to function as a collaborating, representative body for the coordination of all licensure areas. A plan is being developed to increase technological resources for the unit to include an electronics classroom, computers for education faculty, and e-mail access. Two professional clinics conducted by the lead Network consultant were titled "NCATE Overview and Developing an Education

Plan" and "Governance and Collaboration." A third professional clinic, "Designing a Conceptual Framework and Writing an Institutional Report," was jointly conducted by the lead consultant with an external expert. These sessions provided practical applications to identified needs.

The Department of Teacher Education and Interdisciplinary Studies, in conjunction with the Dean of the VUU Business School, the Virginia Department of Education, and local technology consultants, designed on its own and carried out a two-day workshop titled "Exploring the Possibilities of Instructional Technology." As a result of its participation in several national conferences and NCATE training sessions, the department is very conscientiously documenting its progress and efforts to strengthen and improve its operations.

A grant from the Lilly Endowment, Inc., has made it possible for the department to support some of the Arts and Science faculty in attending local, state, and national meetings of interest to teacher education. The department chair and faculty have generated a great deal of interest, enthusiasm, and support for NCATE accreditation. Faculty in Arts and Science have volunteered to serve on the Teacher Education Council and want to be involved in the redesign and restructuring of the program. Participation in the professional clinics has been enthusiastic and meaningful. NCATE accreditation is a goal the department believes in and sees itself accomplishing in an exemplary manner. The trust factor, so critical in the consultant/institutional relationship, could not have been stronger and has been a vital accomplishment.

Virginia Union presents a thorough historical backdrop for viewing its accreditation progress and redefinition of teacher education. Its history has been a catalyst for change. Its development has been effective. Specifically, the fire of 1994 ignited positive action. It was apparent that history and the family approach had led to an infrastructure that superseded physical space and resources. The unit prepared for accreditation without delay.The struggles of Virginia Union and other teacher education programs around the country are both dissimilar and similar. The professional community has not been commonly noted in many teacher education programs, even though the histories of historically Black colleges and universities suggest that professional communities helped teacher education accomplish near-impossible feats more than 80 years ago. The Jeunes Teachers in the South banded together, much like the Virginia Union faculty. Both taught and conducted professional business even without professorial trappings. Both shared space and materials. The learning process and the students were the number one considerations.

One major lesson learned from Virginia Union is that teacher education can be improved with meager resources and physical space. Disasters can occur, but commitment and community can keep the unit moving ahead, doing a lot with a little.

CHAPTER 7

BEYOND THE NETWORK

B. Denise Hawkins
Pauletta B. Bracy
JoAnne S. Drane
Margaret Cole White

This monograph is primarily devoted to selected institutions that have participated in the Historically Black Colleges and Universities Technical Support Network, a joint project of AACTE and NCATE to strengthen teacher preparation at HBCUs. However, there also were institutions outside the Network and its funding sources that nonetheless used Network consultants and services as they sought NCATE accreditation. Mississippi Valley State University was one of those institutions. Its story, and the stories of eight others, is told here.

Since its establishment in 1994, the Network has developed and used a four-phase technical assistance model to help strengthen preparatory programs for P-12 teachers and to support institutions' efforts to become NCATE-accredited. One of the key elements of the model is its team of national consultants, said representatives of many of the institutions that have used the network.

In fact, the most important element in the entire institutional process was intended to be the role of consultants in helping teacher education units strengthen teacher education programs through the pursuit of NCATE accreditation. The project's 12 consultants were selected because of their diverse educational experiences both with HBCUs and with the dynamics of technical assistance and accreditation. As consultants, they have conducted needs assessments at HBCUs in support of quality teacher education programs at those institutions.

In the chapter that follows, we briefly describe the expanded set of institutions that worked with HBCUTSN consultants toward the goal of achieving national accreditation. An extended narrative describing the experience of Mississippi Valley State University is followed by thumbnail sketches of eight other institutions:

Arkansas Baptist College
University of Arkansas at Pine Bluff
Elizabeth City State University
Saint Augustine's College
Tennessee State University
Prairie View A&M University
Clark Atlanta University
Tuskegee University

Mississippi Valley State University, Itta Bena, Mississippi

Since Mississippi Valley State University opened its doors to teachers more than four decades ago, the tiny town of Itta Bena has continued to serve as a convenient marker for this historically Black institution, which many say is really in the middle of nowhere. "Valley" is actually located a mile and a half from Itta Bena, a town of

2,000 Black people. Between Itta Bena and its neighbor Greenwood, just eight miles to the east, are the cotton fields and the catfish farms that produce Mississippi's two major cash crops.

Mississippi Valley is in the Delta, a region still known for agriculture, intense poverty, and racial polarization. Such a glaring backdrop can loom large when a school is known by many in the state as the "smallest, youngest, and Blackest" of Mississippi's eight public universities.

Accreditation and the Undercurrents of a Landmark Legal Battle

When Valley enrolled its first class—all education majors—in 1950, the institution became known in the Delta as a training ground for anyone Black who wanted to become a teacher. Following graduation in those days, teachers were snapped up and dispatched to economically needy Black school districts that dotted the Delta. Today, Black students in the Delta are still in need of Black teachers, and the demand is far from being met. According to state reports, 25 percent of Mississippi's teachers are expected to retire in the next two to three years, the majority of them coming from the Delta. The shortage is growing intense. An aging teacher population, low salaries, and small graduate turnout have chipped away at the supply of teachers, Valley administrators contend.

Since the early 1980s, Valley's mission of growing teachers and maintaining a nationally accredited teacher education program has at times sputtered as the university lost students and amassed a ballooning debt. It also was struggling to stave off the undercurrents of a nasty higher education desegregation battle that threatened its very existence. Tough economic times hit Mississippi hard in the early 1980s. When the state looked for ways to cut costs and shore up its financial base, it cast its eyes on Mississippi Valley. With 28 key academic programs on the chopping block, the cost-cutting proposals resonated like a death knell for education officials.

More than a decade earlier, in 1975, Jake Ayers Sr., and 20 other Black plaintiffs sued the state of Mississippi (*Ayers v. Fordice*) for operating a racially dual system of higher education—a superior one for Whites and a lesser and unequal one for African-Americans. Over the years, attempts to resolve the landmark case have wreaked havoc with Valley's efforts to grow students. The case threatened but did not derail efforts of its education program to maintain accreditation. Valley education officials called the case "a distraction and a disruption, but not a deterrent," to its goal of national accreditation. By 1992, campus enrollment had increased. That was the year that Valley began preparing for reaccreditation of its education program, which was set to lapse in 1996. It also was in 1992 that Valley was dealt a double blow—one from the state and one from NCATE.

In 1992, the *Ayers* case made its way to the U.S. Supreme Court, which ruled in favor of Ayers, saying that the state of Mississippi had not done enough to eliminate the vestiges of segregation in its public universities. When the case was remanded to the U.S. District Court in Oxford, Mississippi, for remedy, Mississippi's Board of Trustees of State Institutions of Higher Learning said that it could not afford eight institutions. The state responded to the Supreme Court ruling in October 1992 by issuing a third controversial closure plan for Valley. With the cloud of closure hanging over Valley, NCATE permitted Valley to delay its on-site accreditation visit. Although the plans to close Valley's doors were eventually defeated, in the interim faculty morale plummeted and enrollment in the teacher education program was derailed.

When the accreditation process resumed two years later, in 1994, Valley officials already knew that the future of the college's professional education program was in deep trouble. The results of a mock accreditation visit revealed more weaknesses than strengths. In early February 1996, there was another setback to national accreditation. The findings of the Board of Examiners' report confirmed what Valley officials needed to do—halt the process and begin anew.

Because Mississippi is a designated "partnership state" that relies on NCATE to accredit teacher education programs before the state issues licenses, Valley officials in March 1996 made a special appeal to NCATE to grant an additional delay. The request was approved, provided that Valley start over immediately in 1997.

The Cloud of Closure

For four years, from 1992 to 1996, the education program lived intimately with the threat of closure while it sought initial accreditation under NCATE's redesign. The climate that existed on campus after the first closure plan lingered like a Mississippi summer. Efforts to recruit and sustain faculty and students seemed to be undermined by stringent, state-imposed admissions standards that took administrators and prospective students by surprise. Recruitment efforts were further impeded by the state's closure plans.

When the accreditation process was launched again in May 1996, Valley officials called on the HBCU Network for help in assessing its efforts and bolstering its chances of success. What Network consultants gave them, say Valley education officials, was "a prescription for relief that we did our best to follow."

When the consultants arrived, they found a unit riddled with problems. As they prepared for the on-site visit in 1996, Valley officials worked unaware of the NCATE standards that had become effective in the fall of 1995. Consultants also found a unit that prepared teachers in a virtual academic vacuum. Limited by a lack of resources and state funding, Valley faculty and the education program had become frightfully sheltered, with little interaction with other professional organizations and institutions of higher learning. Faculty and students did little research and attended few or no conferences. To help get the unit and its faculty back on track and ready for the on-site accreditation visit, Network consultants recommended participation in a series of professional clinics and NCATE workshops in areas including technology, action research, and multiculturalism as they relate to the unit's model. Consultants also assessed each standard for the level of readiness and instituted measures to help empower the faculty.

It was not long before the overhaul got under way. In less than two months, and between the first and second site visits, the vice president for academic affairs revised the faculty evaluation process in the education unit with the goal of placing more emphasis on research and scholarship. The change prompted the use of a new faculty evaluation tool on a university-wide basis. In addition, the Teacher Education Council was instituted to support governance in the teacher education program and coordination of efforts and programs.

The transformation continued among the faculty, who began to take an active role in developing the program's conceptual framework, which focused on teachers as lifelong learners and reflective thinkers.

In 1996, Valley officials enlisted teacher education alumni to support accreditation efforts. Melverta R. Henderson earned both her undergraduate and master's degrees in elementary education from Valley more than 40 years ago, she told the Board of Examiners in her letter. She also told them why an institution like Valley is a necessity: "Mississippi Valley State University is situated in an area where it is most needed... Valley State is here for a reason. It helps young people help themselves. We need the Valley as much today as we did forty-six years ago—if not more."

Voyce C. Morris, special programs supervisor at North Bolivar School District in Shelby,

Mississippi, wrote: "Looming in the midst of the Mississippi Delta cotton fields, Mississippi Valley State University stands as a beacon of hope for many students who endeavor to enrich the quality of their lives through a myriad of program offerings. . . . " Morris implored the BOE to "help us to keep the vision of hope clearly defined through uninterrupted accreditation."

In her letter of support to the BOE, Barbara S. Jones, of Greenville, Mississippi, asked, "Where would I be if Mississippi Valley State University had not been located in Itta Bena, Mississippi, a place accessible to me and my parents? Well, it's hard to say!"

When the BOE's NCATE representative came to visit the Valley community, he posed a similar question to those he met—"What would happen if Valley ceased to exist?" The response he received was a shared, "We wouldn't exist either."

Cause for Survival, "Beacon of Hope"

Following that visit, Valley's teacher education program received an unusual citation for exemplary practice. The citation concluded that Valley was "a small institution of some 2,000 students that represents the only hope that many Delta residents have to escape brutal poverty.... In talking to people in the community, you frequently hear. . . : 'If it hadn't been for Valley....'"

The citation continues, "The magic of Valley is in its people....It is reasonable to expect that all colleges will provide the kind of enabling climate that is provided at Valley and, therefore, not deserving of exemplary notice. However, anyone who spends a day or two at the Valley knows that this is a special place that is deserving of emulation."

Valley has now survived *Ayers*, the fluctuation in student enrollment, increased admissions standards, and NCATE accreditation. Formal notification of NCATE accreditation came in April 1997, just weeks before commencement.

Arkansas Baptist College, Little Rock, Arkansas

Administrators at Arkansas Baptist College sought the help of Network consultants to advise them on preparations for initial accreditation. The first of two visits to the campus was conducted in March 1996. The second served as a follow-up with faculty and staff engaged in preparations for NCATE accreditation and a visit by the Board of Examiners. Central to the follow-up visit were meetings with university administrators and unit faculty and staff to discern the school's readiness for the accreditation process.

Arkansas Baptist College is a small college. Although the entire faculty and staff from all disciplines were eventually involved in the accreditation process, only four full-time faculty reside in teacher education and deliver a single program in elementary education. The college community attended three subsequent meetings with the consultant as focus on the preparation for the official visit continued. The community's ownership of and integral involvement in the process were primary throughout the preparation. Following those sessions with an individual consultant, a mock team visited the campus to assess readiness in a more formal fashion and provided candid feedback. The review process is ongoing.

The University of Arkansas at Pine Bluff, Arkansas

The University of Arkansas at Pine Bluff (UAPB) was a case study with two modifications: adjustments made to the template of the Network process, and a commitment to the university's efforts from a higher level.

First, because of unique circumstances the Network team responded to a request for assistance in preparing for accreditation following a successful appeal—the team's protocol shifted to focus on the work previously completed and make recommendations to enhance overall presentation in both the institutional report and documentation. In a sense, all four stages of the template were dealt with concurrently throughout the process.

The president of the University of Arkansas system, Alan Sugg, was keenly interested in UAPB's attempts to seek NCATE accreditation. He met with the mock team on the campus and assured support and necessary resources to assist UAPB. He said he intended to have UAPB recognized as a premier institution for teacher education in the state.

Network consultants were dispatched to UAPB after the institution had been denied accreditation, then later granted a second visit. "The Network team is critical to any HBCU preparing for accreditation," declared Calvin Johnson, dean of the School of Education. During their February 1, 1995, visit to the university, consultants served on a mock team and provided feedback for each of the accreditation standards. During their subsequent visits to the campus, they monitored progress, made recommendations, and assisted the faculty with drafting key reports. Their presence, Johnson said, was essential to enlisting the support of both university administrators and unit faculty members in the accreditation process.

Network consultants also served as the spur that many faculty members in the unit needed to take ownership of the accreditation process. "There was no resistance to the NCATE process from the university administration, but that was not the case with faculty," Johnson said. "Their participation in the accreditation process made them realize that they were members of the university team" responsible for making NCATE accreditation a reality.

Elizabeth City State University, Elizabeth City, North Carolina, and Saint Augustine's College, Raleigh, North Carolina

We want to obtain initial national accreditation! The CEO of the institution, department chairpersons, faculty, and students agreed that the quest was essential to the healthy existence of the institution in fulfilling its mission. Now the quest begins. The unanimity of thought—how to, who will, where is, who is—ends.

To facilitate this quest, a new model emerged. During the 1990s, through the combined efforts of NCATE and AACTE and the demonstrated success of some HBCUs, a new format developed that assisted other HCBUs in obtaining initial national accreditation. Having worked through the accreditation process at Elizabeth City State University, a Network consultant was able to assist St. Augustine's College in its quest.

At both institutions, a Network consultant helped the schools of education address a common concern that is critical to the accreditation process—the need to maintain written documents and records. "At HCBUs, especially in the case of smaller ones, there is a strong reliance on oral history, but the accreditation process requires written and ongoing documentation," the consultant found. Retrieving documents, such as those on governance policies, was nothing short of detective work, the consultant reported. In two instances, the consultant's quest successfully ended with a campus archivist not affiliated with the teacher education unit. "Fortunately, the archivist had a long history with the institution and knew the history of the unit," the consultant said.

Now that computers are readily available everywhere, effective strategies for maintaining and revising documents can be put in place. "For HBCUs, what really needs to be put in place is a known and singular repository for department documents," the consultant suggested. "Documents should carry an update and revise date in the computer. They should also be disseminated to involved persons—give them a hard copy and an electronic version."

Tennessee State University, Nashville, Tennessee

When Network consultants were invited to Tennessee State University (TSU), they were told to be "brutally honest" in their assessment and recommendations to help the unit prepare for the day when the "real team arrived." The university and the faculty got what they asked for, said Franklin Jones, dean of the College of Education at TSU. "They helped us get our house in order in a positive and comprehensive way."

In addition to providing the unit with an honest and candid assessment of written and oral responses to NCATE standards, the three Network consultants chose to share with the institution any and all perceived problems and concerns (no matter how small) related to the unit's overall readiness for NCATE accreditation. This resulted in commentary for 16 of the 20 standards under review. General recommendations pertinent to a wide variety of issues, including strategies for monitoring the progress of task completions and accomplishments, also were included.

In preparing for accreditation, the College of Education at TSU was able to use to advantage a number of its strong characteristics such as good facilities, student and faculty diversity, and professional community collaboration. Most important to TSU's success in achieving accreditation was the emphatic support of TSU's president, who made quite clear what his expectations were regarding full accreditation for all credible programs on the campus, and was invaluable in mobilizing faculty.

Prairie View A&M University, Prairie View, Texas

The Network has made an outstanding contribution to the accreditation process, declared Dr. Mohinder Paul Mehta, dean of the College of

Education at Prairie View A&M University. Network consultants, he added, "helped us by suggesting rewrites and how best to use data and how to enhance document presentation."

There were several other areas in which Network consultants were helpful: generating support for increasing the number of faculty in the unit for advanced-level programs, identifying the need for clear differentiation between initial and advanced-level programs, serving as the impetus for clarification of unit governance procedures and processes, and recommending clearer connections between the conceptual framework and student outcomes.

Helping Prairie View faculty to appreciate, understand, and value NCATE's emphasis on "the unit," not on the individual programs that comprise the unit, was a challenge for Network consultants. This situation was not unique to Prairie View, however. Network consultants have discovered that when individual programs hold accreditation or special credentials from their respective specialties, there is sometimes a tendency for these units' faculty to speak from a less unit-oriented focus and to be more narrowly program-specific. Apparently this concern was dealt with and did not carry over to the actual NCATE visit, held some months after the Network team's review.

Clark Atlanta University, Atlanta, Georgia

At Clark Atlanta University, a larger university with several graduate programs, the School of Education committed the university to the process of seeking accreditation by involving broad-based representation from across disciplines, including other professional schools. Faculty from other disciplines attended briefings, served on writing teams, and were studiously kept abreast of developments. Another group directly involved in the process were members of the National Visiting Committee, an advisory board of practitioners and experts in the field of education assembled annually to advise the School of Education and university administration. The 1997 committee focused on NCATE and provided a forum for members to respond to standards with fresh perspectives from the world of practice. Collaboration and a spirit of shared responsibility in both situations were apparent.

Tuskegee University, Alabama

Tuskegee University was seeking continued accreditation when two Network consultants were assigned to assist the College of Education. Before their visit, a reorganization had occurred that merged the College of Education and the College of Liberal Arts. The newly appointed dean had held an appointment in the Department of English and was now faced with the tasks of facilitating the merger and preparing for the NCATE visit. This innovative situation posed a new challenge for both faculties and was deemed a compelling opportunity to strengthen articulation between the two former units. It was quite a successful venture, and now serves as a model for a productive relationship between liberal arts and education.

Part II

PATHWAYS TO CHANGE

"Where there is no vision the people will perish"
Proverbs 29:18

CHAPTER 8

LESSONS FOR THE PROFESSIONAL COMMUNITY

Carol E. Smith
Cynthia J. Graddy

[T]he concept of professional community and its implications suffuse NCATE's standards. . . .Teacher education's purpose and identity emanate from the fundamental task of improving learning opportunities for all learners. When education units see their purpose as derived from the larger collaborative goals, their sense of professional community becomes a crucial element in realizing the goals (Capturing the Vision).

Despite the best efforts of standards designers, the climate of 1990s education reform has brought connotations to the word "standard" such as stringent, accountable, or mandated. The term "collaboration" is associated with concepts such as teamwork, communication, and shared values. Building bridges between these two concepts has been the work and the nature of the networks forged by institutions in the HBCU Technical Support Network.

How are these connections made? How can the dynamic of an "in the family," collegially based relationship be juxtaposed with the external evaluation of accreditation review? How does the goal of reaching all students at the P-12 level empower teacher educators to think inclusively about all institutions? Studies in the preceding chapters describe journeys by closely knit groups of faculty to reach a goal whose achievement would ultimately be judged by outsiders. Despite this challenge, the process worked—as it does in other institutions across the country—because faculty in the institution, consultants, and reviewers shared a common language and set of goals.

The *lingua franca* began to emerge as institutions worked through the needs assessment process required by NCATE standards. It gradually developed into a much richer shared language of understandings about institutional context, local communities, and common goals. In the process, Network consultants became a sort of adjunct faculty as they worked with their colleagues to strengthen program quality and develop better presentations of evidence. At the same time, teacher education faculty began to develop the capacity to evaluate themselves from an external perspective— using the lens that the NCATE reviewers develop for making judgments based on national standards and norms.

This interplay between the push toward standards and the need to collaborate is one of the major themes of this story. It is even reflected in the title of this volume: "Reforming teacher education through accreditation" and "telling our story" are part of two distinct contexts that converged in the Network. Its variations are an important part of what makes the Network professionally successful and personally rewarding for faculty, consultants, and project staff.

The Current Context of Education Standards for Historically Black Institutions

All teacher preparation institutions now face an environment of accountability and increasing external evaluation as education reform efforts that grew out of the report A Nation at Risk continue to result in a growing array of standards and new performance expectations at both P-12 and higher education levels. The increasing focus on performance-based licensure, certification, and accreditation standards is paralleled by the explosion of discipline-based national standards for student performance, assessment, and curriculum.

The traditional underfunding of HBCUs does not protect them from increasingly higher standards for teacher education. Indeed, the standards-based environment of the 1980s and 1990s presents special challenges to the preparation of African-American teachers as a new set of influences begins to shape the environment in which teacher educators and their teaching candidates must operate:

- New forms of licensure have the potential to extend the length of teacher preparation programs and thereby increase the costs to the candidate. Because student costs are important factors for HBCUs, undergraduate choices (Wenglinsky 1997 ETS monograph on HBCUs, p. 3), could motivate students to bypass teaching for other programs of study.

- The move toward new forms of performance assessment for state licensure and professional certification will most likely mean that beginning and practicing teachers face increased costs for basic credentialing required to teach; unlike the costs of pre-service preparation, these costs are not eligible for subsidy by federal financial aid or other forms of undergraduate support.

- The concerns with the adverse impact of emerging performance assessments for teachers have not yet been adequately addressed: "authentic" performance measures may reflect equity problems in terms of standards, assessment design, and scoring (Jordan-Irvine Fraser, 1998). The effect of such adverse impact in assessment will reach to the institutions that prepare teachers as well as the candidates themselves.

- The emphasis on outcomes in teacher assessment carries with it potential incentives for teacher preparation institutions to select those students who are already well prepared to meet performance standards (Diez 1997). The same incentives may operate with respect to P-12 schools in which teacher candidates are placed, because student learning is an increasingly important element of the evaluation of teacher effectiveness.

- Inclusion of expectations around technology in every type of education standard and related assessment threatens to worsen the already uneven playing field for HBCUs as higher education institutions struggle to support the necessary expenditures, and prospective teachers find their clinical and internship experiences located in schools that may not be equipped to meet technological expectations.

• Historically Black colleges and universities are located primarily in the southeastern United States, where the combination of lower school funding and traditional state assessment policy has led to a cycle that includes heavy use of high-stakes testing in schools. The resulting impact is a sometimes damaging form of accountability that operates within the schools in which many African-American teachers will be prepared and ultimately assigned (Neill, 1977).

Collaboration as a Challenge and a Solution

Seen from the vantage point of potential threats posed by this "new accountability" environment, becoming part of the HBCU Network effort at first seems a counter-intuitive move. Why would institutions that had not previously sought accreditation embrace an external review under conditions far more challenging than many other institutions face? What did they hope to achieve, and how were they able to envision this effort as one with positive outcomes?

There were probably at least two dimensions that attracted faculty in Network institutions to undertake this challenge. The first is the natural curiosity to find out where one's institution rates on the scale. Certainly, the use of a forceful needs assessment process at the very beginning appealed to faculty risk-takers who were willing to engage in a wide-ranging conversation that included both external consultants and members of their own central administration. A second element that attracted faculty (and perhaps helped to counterbalance the risks associated with public evaluation) was the presentation of NCATE standards by consultants and project staff as a conceptual framework that promoted the central values and mission held by these institutions.

NCATE's standards focus on elements that are central to the traditional effort of HBCUs to strengthen their role in assuring high-quality preparation of African-American teachers:

1. *Resources* are directly addressed: Support for the professional development of students and faculty, as well as academic and personnel support, are explicitly evaluated in the NCATE review process. Where resources are not adequate to meet the increasing expectations for professional preparation, NCATE helps the teacher education program to make a well-documented statement of those shortcomings and to advocate for more appropriate support (NCATE Standards, second printing 97).

2. *Diversity* as a value permeates the NCATE standards and is a fundamental element of NCATE's own conceptual framework. The

standards language has a broad focus that includes several dimensions—diversity as an educational value, student and faculty diversity reflecting American life, affirmative action to support access to education, and diversity as an essential element of teacher preparation (NCATE 1994).

3. *Professional community* is a theme throughout the NCATE standards that connects the preparation of a diverse teaching force to collegial work within the institution and in P-12 schools. Again, NCATE's scope is a broad one, encompassing teacher educators, teacher candidates, liberal arts faculty, P-12 practitioners, and others. The strong focus on community outreach through P-16 faculty's academic and professional work has a long history in the African-American community, and is reinforced by many education policy initiatives now promoting such dimensions as service learning and integrated service preparation for candidates in the professions.

The focus on professional community formed the bridge between NCATE standards and the kind of collaboration that impelled faculty in the HBCU Network institutions to engage in this process. NCATE's professional community standard speaks of collaboration as a force to renew effective teacher preparation and to improve the quality of education in P-12 schools. Collaboration not only became the adhesive that made the HBCU Network operation effective, but also served as the link to a vital goal that all faculty could share: improving educational quality for learners traditionally underserved by systems of standards and accountability.

As previously noted, HBCUs are usually resource-poor, a condition reflected in reduced faculty, technology, and general support for academic programs. Although it may be an impetus for rethinking program design, lack of resources also can undermine any attempts to restructure and improve the quality of programs. Hence, sharing resources is an obvious way to enhance programs without expanding the associated operating budget.

Internal collaboration is the first step for institutions. Boyer notes that "professors, to be fully effective, cannot work continuously in isolation. Scholarship at its best should bring faculty together" (Boyer, 1977). Shared human resources—whether faculty meetings or professional clinics—allow for shared knowledge, shared physical resources, and streamlined practices. Location and technology challenges made external collaboration somewhat more difficult for institutions in the Network, but as faculty members began to share their work outside of their own institutions, the benefits were immediate. Sharing of program renewal efforts with other HBCUs allowed the Network institutions to strengthen their own knowledge and commitment. Communication with faculty at national conferences helped institutions to learn from the struggles of others.

All facets of the Network model rely heavily on the collaborative approach and spirit. An in-depth self-study cannot be performed without assistance from arts and sciences faculty and the teacher education students. The educative phase of the

Network model cannot be carried out effectively without knowledgeable external resources. Faculty in the institution cannot be coaches or be coached themselves without being receptive to new ideas developed outside of the familiar realm.

The Network also has allowed the participating HBCUs to explore the impact of national reforms and restructuring efforts on their programs. Participants were briefed through workshop sessions, newsletters, and updates on how national standards organizations are developing criteria, standards, indicators, principles, and goals relating to the improvement of all teachers and teacher education programs. Members of the Network faculty have been directly involved with boards, committees, and task forces dealing with these issues. Not only are they beginning to adapt their programs to these strategies and educating their colleagues within the institution, but they are educating colleagues in the broader education community through their direct involvement in standards-setting efforts. Again, the collaborative focus supports the effort to meet continually higher standards.

Finding Lessons in Our Own Stories

Evaluating one's own work is always difficult, but the need to reflect on one's practice is a foundation of good teaching and teacher education. What benefit has the Network provided for the HBCUs that participated in this project, and for the role of HBCUs in their historic mission? What have we learned that could be of use to other institutions and the broader education community? What lessons can these institutions provide that will benefit the larger agenda of education reform?

The Supreme Court's decision in *U.S. v. Fordice* (1992) stated that HBCUs are a vestige of segregation and state legislatures must either eliminate them or find educational justification for their existence. The survival of historically Black colleges and universities depends increasingly on showing that they provide education benefits not otherwise available (ETS, 1997). Opening chapters of this publication have described the long history of HBCUs in producing Black community leaders and public figures; educating teachers and social workers for the Black community; and more recently broadening the professional avenues for Black students in professions and the sciences. Their role in providing more affordable and accessible higher education opportunities for Blacks also has been documented (ETS, 1997). The benefits of HBCUs to the Black community are clear, even more so when one considers the field of teacher preparation: almost half of all Black teacher education students are prepared at HBCUs, an increasingly diverse P-12 student population requires greater diversity in the teacher workforce, and steadily increasing enrollment on HBCU campuses indicates that they are filling a clear need (ETS, 1997).

One reason for the formation of the HBCU Network was to sustain the crucial role of HBCUs in recruiting and developing the next generation of Black teachers. The impact of the Network's efforts to date can be seen in the strengthening of teacher education programs for these participating institutions:

• By selecting a consultant cadre that represents

a variety of education experiences and backgrounds, the Network provided a rich resource base for HBCUs and other institutions interested in program quality improvement and/or national accreditation review.

- Lead consultants for the Network created the assessment process for HBCUs. Therefore, they were able to provide firsthand experience with the rationale for particular elements of the model.

- Network consultants and staff were kept current on education-related events through briefings, newsletters, and seminars so they could better inform HBCUs on the relationship between program quality review measures and education reform participants such as NBPTS or INTASC.

- Collaborative networks built internally (i.e., arts and sciences and the teacher preparation department) not only helped HBCUs prepare for NCATE, but also strengthened the relationship between pedagogy and content knowledge at a time when state teacher licensure systems place increased emphasis on this connection in teachers' demonstrated performance.

- The influence of HBCUs and their faculty in the national dialogue on education reform increased as consultants and faculty began to serve as leaders in national conferences on standards and student learning.

These successes fulfill the first part of the HBCU Network's intended purpose. But what are the benefits and lessons for majority institutions? Is the HBCU Network a closed enterprise that cannot be extended to others in the education community? Consultants who provided the primary leadership for this Network suggest otherwise. An important part of telling the story is ensuring that the lessons learned are shared with the wider professional community. The context for these lessons is important:

• *Some lessons are based on consulting with majority institutions.* HBCU consultants who readied themselves to respond to requests from majority institutions found that, regardless of their economic, demographic, and geographic situation of the institutions, the general needs were similar— clear and concise suggestions from consultants (including sensitive areas); knowledgeable and reliable advice on sources of expertise; feasible solutions in the particular context of a given institution; and continued assistance from the original consultant as the faculty wrestled with new challenges. Network institutions may have adapted more easily than some other institutions to the challenges inherent in a consulting relationship— sharing "dirty laundry" with outsiders, undergoing continual external reviews, remaining open to the suggestion that there are other methods of operation.

• *Other lessons emerged from observations of HBCUs and their method of operation.* Network consultants were not surprised with what they found in majority institutions because underlying positives and negatives often were very similar to those found in HBCUs. On the plus side, institutions often demonstrated nurturing environments for their students, a committed faculty, and a sense of urgency in addressing new expectations for teacher preparation. On the minus side, lack of resources often was a problem for specific program areas even in more adequately funded institutions; many institutions did not have adequate documentation, relying instead on oral history or personal knowledge of individual faculty members. In addition, lack of adequate communication among faculty across the teacher preparation enterprise is a virtually universal problem that plagues all types of institutions.

Thus, the lessons start from a common base of shared obstacles and advantages. What can be distilled from the Network's struggles, successes, and continuing challenges?

1. **Addressing NCATE standards helped the institution do what it needed to do anyway to strengthen its teacher preparation.** Authors of the Xavier chapter, for instance, note:

We recognized strong parallels between some of our program weaknesses (identified through surveying nearly 1,200 individuals, including Xavier pre-service and in-service teachers, principals, counselors, and other education stakeholders in the community, and through external evaluators) and the themes that would guide our institutional assessment for NCATE readiness.

Authors of the chapter on LeMoyne-Owen's experience also note the link between their willingness to take on the NCATE task and the results of earlier program reviews conducted by the state, identifying weaknesses that they saw as linked to some of the program resources described in NCATE standards.

2. **The resource issue can be maneuvered, but ultimately it cannot be bypassed.** In many of the participating institutions, underfunding and lack of adequate resources were a significant challenge. Initial needs assessment reports described teacher preparation programs that had survived and continued to operate despite a long-standing and chronic dearth of basic resources. In many cases, extraordinary faculty commitment was the basis upon which the teacher education program had continued to run, with faculty carrying continuous overloads and contributing personal time and resources to keep the program running.

In some cases, the missing resource base could be finessed by creative management and continued personal support from the faculty. But increasingly, external accountability (for instance, state licensure standards) and the expectations exerted by NCATE and other professional standards turn the spotlight on deficiencies caused by lack of adequate financial support for teacher preparation. HBCUs are certainly not the only institutions for which this problem is acute, although the underfunding of teacher education in HBCUs may be more likely to stem from historic underfunding of the institution rather than under-allocation within the institution.

In the case of NCATE review, inadequate resources will be specifically identifiable because the standards explicitly address adequacy of resources. In the case of licensure standards, the consequences of underfunding may be more insidious, if they are reflected in poor performance of teacher candidates whose opportunity to learn has not been adequately supported. This is a serious issue for higher education faculty and state policymakers who must ensure that public accountability does not become a slogan that allows perpetuation of historic discrimination in financing of higher education.

3. **Parts of the NCATE process are challenging because they require institutions to examine basic beliefs and values.** This is especially true as institutions design their conceptual frameworks. Many of the case studies in this monograph relate challenges of developing conceptual framework language that was appropriate to the philosophy and design of a teacher education program, and that also met NCATE requirements concerning the base of knowledge and research. The conceptual framework "is the 'rudder' that steers the entire ship," the Xavier chroniclers found. In

the case of Delaware State University, conceptual framework and knowledge base questions also arose at the beginning and had to be addressed before the other pieces could really fall into place.

Such problems can be both the most vexing and the most valuable pieces of the NCATE process because they require the faculty to dig to the very foundations of their beliefs and mission and to establish or re-establish the building blocks on which all else rests. In the case of Xavier, for instance, revisiting the original mission resulted in a conceptual framework that extends beyond professional standards to reaffirm the cultural and religious heritage at the core of the institution's foundation.

4. **The factor of time is easily underestimated.** Network institutions, like most others, began the project with an assumption that two years would be required to prepare for NCATE review. Some institutions were able to complete the preparations within this time frame, but even they experienced unpredictable events that threatened to delay the process. For most institutions, the needs assessment was the first concrete product to emerge from this time period. One of the main challenges was to keep moving fast enough to reach the appointment with NCATE on time, while also planning adequate time for substantive faculty discussions that would likely create some change in direction.

Organization and management of time was a very important dimension. Howard University's authors describe their approach to holding a year of weekly meetings and including summer time that would otherwise have represented unproductive downtime for the faculty. Scheduling of professional clinics was another challenge for institutions with heavy teaching loads; faculty found it difficult to coordinate time together for the serious discussions that needed to accompany documentation of the conceptual framework standards.

Adding to the concerns about time, most of the Network institutions experienced significant leadership changes during the evaluation period (see, for example, the description of changes at Virginia Union University, Delaware State University, and LeMoyne-Owen College). This situation added to the potential for confusion and delay. To stay within reach of the original timeline, it became very important to have some core of faculty who stayed in place with a common sense of purpose. For institutions such as Mississippi Valley State University and Arkansas Baptist College—operating under a state deadline to retain accreditation—managing the time factors became critical to survival.

5. **The accreditation process is enhanced when external review becomes an ongoing effort.** Institutions often tend to

think of NCATE review as a process of intense effort within the institution followed by a single external review that tells faculty whether they got it right. Because the model created for the Network began with external review even before NCATE preparations were initiated, it created a collegial bond between institutional faculty and a group of outsiders from the very start. Although the potential for immediate discomfort resulted from use of a discrepancy analysis model, the ultimate benefit of this approach was to sharpen the faculty's ability to analyze problems and challenges. Virginia Union's account indicates that faculty had accurately identified program areas for improvement, "but it was not . . . until these findings were reported by the (Network) consultant team that the teacher education administrators realized what the staff and faculty had been saying all along about the program areas that needed improvement." Here, as in the case of Howard University, the external review via a needs assessment process provided leverage for change.

Faculty in Network institutions had relatively little difficulty in analyzing their own program needs once the appropriate framework was set for this effort. The upsets caused by the rigor of an initial needs assessment were more than offset by the sense among faculty that they had already been through the worst and had a very good sense of how NCATE would view the professional education unit. Study after study in this monograph describes an expression of initial dismay by the faculty, followed by a roll-up-the-sleeves effort to pull together toward completing the self-study. Continuing reviews (professional clinics, mock visits, and other formats) served as benchmarks along the way to mark progress and highlight goals remaining to be met. This approach not only provided enormous help to the institutions in preparing for NCATE review, but in the process created a living example of "professional community."

What lessons were learned with respect to the importance of collaboration in the HBCU Network effort? While collaboration was initially seen as the final phase of the Network model, faculty in this project learned that collaboration was in fact the only effective way to reach the final stage. The following observations reflect some of these lessons:

1. **Bureaucratic modes of operating and organizing can be an obstacle to collaboration.** From its outset, the HBCU Network project dealt with ordinary and extraordinary problems caused by organizational structures that impeded progress. Every aspect, from basic communication to significant decision-making, was influenced by the nature of internal operations. For instance, lead faculty in the Network institutions sometimes expressed surprise at certain NCATE requirements or specific documents

that needed to be submitted (and sometimes were already overdue). The problem often resulted from an arrangement in which the individual in authority (i.e., designated to receive and send communications to NCATE) was entirely separate in the organizational structure from the person actually responsible for carrying out the function.

One dimension of the role played by Network consultants with each of the institutions (minority and majority) was an effort to help the institution and its teacher education program create more effective ways of communicating and achieving goals—sometimes helping to shape an informal structure that proved more effective for accomplishing the work in a collaborative manner.

2. **Lack of communication is both a symptom and a cause of lack of collaboration.** At the beginning, work in some institutions was hindered because basic materials and work products were not shared among individual members of an institution's faculty. This was not intentional hoarding, but the continuation of an ingrained mode in which each faculty member is considered responsible for his or her own information, resources, and work products. The problem was further illustrated and exacerbated when faculty members called the central project office for items that were sitting next door on a colleague's desk, rather than setting up communication within the department.

The character of an individual rather than group or team model of thinking and working threatens to perpetuate itself even in the midst of processes that are intended to be collaborative. The consultant's observations on Delaware State's efforts refer to this problem when, for example, faculty have been out of the loop on the accreditation process for extended periods of time. Communication is key to changing this mode of operating and creating a more collegial approach, and institutional pathways need to be created and nurtured for this communication. The role that external consultants may serve in such situations is not only to help the institution with the substance of its documentation, but to help create the communication processes that allow the faculty to function more effectively.

3. **Institutional needs and problems are not an obstacle to collaboration,** but rather a primary reason for collaborating. Boyce Williams refers to the concept of needs-based collaboration. Institutions in the HBCU Network did not wait until they had it all right to begin working with each other— in fact, their need to address problems was a primary force compelling them to work together. Rather than proving embarrassing, the collaborative effort is what finally allowed many of the Network institutions to address problems they had tried unsuccessfully to address on their own. In Virginia Union's case, collaboration in its extreme form (sharing cramped quarters

after a fire) enabled faculty to rebuild in very short order and keep the NCATE preparations on track at the same time. The LeMoyne-Owen and Doane College exchange became a way of improving the preparation of both colleges' candidates for diverse settings and meeting the NCATE diversity standards in a way neither institution would have been able to do on its own. In the process, faculty from the two institutions were able to establish a dialogue about diversity that enriches both programs.

4. **Collaboration can take many forms and can become a value in itself.** The needs assessment process was the first visible piece of the HBCU Network model seen by the faculty, and it demonstrated collaboration from internal and external perspectives. It is interesting to note that, by the end of their NCATE preparation, consultation had become such a valued resource that institutions looked for every possible way to connect with their consultants—whether through a second needs assessment visit; professional clinics; or meetings at AACTE, NCATE, or other conferences. Delaware State University described its use of a second needs assessment review as providing "much more of a map for program improvement" than the first review had been able to do.

These institutions also expanded their collaborative efforts, extending them far beyond the outlines of their NCATE work. They indicated that collaboration itself was one of the skills they learned. The Xavier authors refer to the process of working with technical support and mentoring as similar to concocting a good gumbo—difficult on the first try. Faculty in institutions must consciously value the process of collaboration enough to work through successive approximations so as to arrive at the style of interactive exchange that works for their own context and needs.

The institutions involved in this effort felt that it was important to communicate their stories. This desire stems in part from the instinct to tell your own story so that others will hear the messages firsthand. But more important, these institutions felt compelled to continue a tradition strong in the African-American community: a concern for the next generation (here in particular, the next generation of educators). It is a determination, as the Xavier authors describe it, to pass on to subsequent generations the values, culture, spirituality, knowledge, and skills that have sustained the people and the efforts that this book honors.

REFERENCES

Boyer, E.L. (1997) *Scholarship Reconsidered : Priorities of the Professoriate.* Princeton, N.J: Carnegie Foundation for the Advancement of Teaching.

Diez, M.E. (1997). *Assessment is Not Enough: The Moral Call for Coherence.* AACTE Briefs, 18(9).

Gideonse, H.D., Ducharme, E.R., Ducharme, M.K., Gollnick, D.M., Lilly, M.S., Shelke, E.L., & Smith, P.E.(1993. *Capturing the Vision: Reflections on NCATE's Redesign Five Years After.* Washington, D.C.: American Association of Colleges for Teacher Education.

Jordan-Irvine, J., & Fraser, J.W. (1998). *'Warm Demanders': Do National Certification Standards Leave Room for the Culturally Responsive Pedagogy of African-American Teachers?* Education Week, 17(35).

National Council for Accreditation of Teacher Education. (1994). *Handbook for Board of Examiners Teams.* Washington, DC: Author.

National Council for Accreditation of Teacher Education. (1997). *Standards, Procedures & Policies for the Accreditation of Professional Education Units.* Washington, DC: Author.

Neill, M. (1997). *Testing Our Children: A Report Card on State Assessment Systems.* Cambridge, MA: National Center for Fair & Open Testing.

Wenglinsky, H. (1997). *Students at Historically Black Colleges and Universities: Their Aspirations & Accomplishments.* Princeton, NJ: Educational Testing Service.

CHAPTER 9

DIRECTIONS FOR THE NETWORK

Boyce C. Williams

We began this discussion of ways to utilize the accreditation process as a means of reforming teacher education programs at Historically Black Colleges and Universities. From the past to the present, collaboratives have served the HBCUs well. Collaboration is a theme that has resurfaced in virtually all the cases, as well as in other discussions. As we look to the future of the Network, the collaboration theme emerges again. Rather than as a by-product of other more focused goals, collaboration is expected to become a major goal, one that is manifested strategically as a plan. In this final chapter, we focus on collaboration—the barriers and the promises for extending each of the major components of the Network model. The chapter ends with a set of guiding principles for developing strategic plans for collaboration.

Barriers

Collaboration has become a buzzword in recent discussions of educational reform. To realize the benefits, we must, however, remove the obstacles that have prevented collaborative efforts from being successful. One obstacle is the practice of working independently, rather than interdependently, even when the goals of different organizations or different units within a single organization are similar. Barth (1996) likens our non-collaborative tendencies to the "parallel play" of children:

> Two three-year-olds are busily engaged in opposite corners of a sandbox. One has a shovel and bucket; one has a rake and hoe. At no time do they share each other's tools. Although in proximity and having much to offer one another, each works and plans pretty much in isolation. (1996:6)

A second obstacle is the absence of collegiality. Robinson (1996) sees the lack of collegiality as reflecting misplaced priorities. He argues that a new kind of collegiality is needed to overcome institutionalized separations borne of difference in status. His discussion makes clear the importance of the human side of things, not only for colleagues in colleges and schools, but also in our work with students. To a great extent the age-old problem of gaps between knowledge and theory, or research and practice can be attributed to failures to collaborate in matters that are obviously related. Barth (1996) calls for dual citizenship for teachers and teacher educators in schools and colleges, arguing that collaboration in the teaching of pre-service professionals will serve to bridge gaps between what students are taught and their application of that knowledge in classroom practice. In a very practical sense, the traditional reward system of higher education is still another obstacle. Colleges inadvertently discourage partnerships with and services to P-12 schools by assigning low status to those who work with them. This environment makes it difficult to sustain collaborative relationships. To reduce the barriers to collaboration, the Network found it useful to redefine collaboration.

It is important to differentiate between the past experiences of HBCUs with collaborative ventures and the types of ventures that the collaborative component of the HBCUTSN model envisioned. Redefining collaboration was an important first step:

> Collaboration is a much used and abused word. Unexamined, it suggests that whatever tasks are to be done can be done equally well by all participants. ... We mean neither an unthinking acceptance of the view that all partners in an activity are equally fit to do all things, nor an elitist view that one group has wisdom and experience superior to the other. We posit an idea yet to be realized: collaboration that capitalizes on the research and experience of the best professors in the academy and on the expertise and experience of the best teachers in the schools, recognizing that valuable attributes reside in both places. (HBCUTSN Handbook, p.64)

This definition distinguishes past experiences with and cooperative initiatives from current ones by calling attention to the need for a proactive stance in planning collaboratives for excellence. The essential goal of collaboration in the HBCUTSN model is to facilitate the process of situating HBCUs for interdependent work and encouraging self-sufficiency. Undergirding the proactive stance advocated here are the beliefs that

1) Collaboration must be planned.
2) Collaborative activities must have a shared vision.
3) Collaborative activities must have a shared language.
4) Collaboration is built on trust and understanding.

Directions for Extending the Model

The needs assessment component of the network existed at two levels: the literal or functional needs identified through direct investigation and review of evidence during the needs assessment process was the first. This was underpinned by a larger general need for building the fundamental capacity that would enable the unit to remedy identified weaknesses. At a fundamental level, an analysis of NCATE accreditation standards often not met by HBCUs reveals five critical areas for future attention: 1) Resources, 2) Faculty Qualifications, 3) Faculty Development, 4) Relationships with Schools, and 5) Faculty Load. At the capacity level, consultants found that institutions needed to strengthen three major dimensions of their programs: 1) developing resources, 2) developing professional networks, and 3) developing professional foundations. These areas inform directions for extending the Network Model.

Developing Resources. Resource Development is linked to the assessment phase of the HBCUTSN facilitation model. The assessment phase helps identify areas in which program elements and program documentation need to be revised or strengthened. It also helps create consensus among faculty within and outside of the professional education unit on the rationale for and direction of needed changes.

We may examine some of the problems that are attributed to limited resources and consider ways that strategic planning for collaboration could aid them: a) recruitment, admission, retention, and career placement of teacher candidates; b) employability problems associated with testing for admission and certification; and c) documentation problems that are undergirded by inadequacies in information management systems for storing, retrieving, and using data for reporting and assessing progress of students and programs. It is clear that **a strategic plan for collaboration ought to include collaboration across units that allows the teacher education unit to capitalize on existing resources of other units whose functions overlap with those of the teacher education unit, e.g., recruiting, admissions, assessment, counseling, and career placement services.**

As noted previously, external resources are too often considered the venue of the Office of Development. The teacher education unit should work closely with the Office of Development in its search for external funds. The teacher education unit should be able to communicate its needs and assist the development officers in writing proposals that address the goals and needs of the unit. Three problems are quite striking. One is that in the past, funding opportunities for teacher education programs have not been attractive to development officials, as the amount of money allocated in the area of teacher education has often been low in comparison to other academic areas. The second is that where funds are more plentiful, for example, in math and science education, professionals in the content disciplines, rather than teacher-educators who focus on the pedagogy of the content, often are selected to play the lead role in projects. The third is that when funds are secured without appropriate communication with the teacher education unit, the nature of the funded projects may not be in keeping with the goals of the unit, resulting in add-ons that increase the workload of an already understaffed area. Larger institutions often resolve these problems by establishing full-time positions for development professionals. This is difficult for smaller institutions. **A strategic plan for collaboration must consider ways to strengthen communication about the teacher education program and to foster collaboratives between teacher education units and development offices for joint resource development activities. Minimally, such a plan would include mechanisms for ensuring that the acquisition of external funds supports the goals and conceptual framework of the teacher education unit.**

Developing Professional Networks. In the educative phase of the model, special attention is given to professional development activities. These are driven largely by areas identified in the needs assessment. Beyond the basics of reviewing the curriculum and initiating faculty development activities for the teacher education unit, the collaboration component focuses on building professional communities to support the ongoing process of learning. Emphasis is placed on establishing systems for continuous development in curriculum restructuring, professional development, and linkages between knowledge and practice. The underlying assumptions are that 1) the teacher education knowledge base is and will always be in a continual state of growth and 2) educators will be continuously involved in advancing the knowledge base for teaching.

It is no secret that concerns about the quality of instruction in schools are directly related to the quality of teachers that teacher education programs produce. As noted by Goodlad (1990), for reform efforts to be successful, we must have "simultaneous renewal" of schools and teacher preparation programs. The move toward simultaneous renewal is undergirded by the recognition of the two-dimensional nature of curriculum restructuring and professional development. The professional network element of collaboration uses the axiom, "Practice What You Teach and Teach What You Practice." In other words, restructuring the curriculum carries with it the obligation for teacher educators to demonstrate the use of those effective practices that they talk about. It has often been said that students are more likely to teach as they were taught than to teach as they were taught to teach. If we restructure teacher education programs, we also must provide opportunities for professional development so that faculty can deliver effective instruction. Of particular interest then are 1) joint professional development and curriculum development programs within the institution, particularly between the teacher education unit and academic units in the arts and sciences, and 2) the development of professional networks between teacher educators and teachers.

In terms of joint professional development and curriculum restructuring, the work on learning communities provides models for adaptation most compatible with the major design features of the collaboration model presented here. Evolving models of learning communities embrace basic concepts associated with contemporary pedagogical reform efforts. Further learning communities may be created for both curriculum development and professional development. By their very nature, learning communities embrace the notions of cooperation, coordination, and communication (Gablenick, et al. (1990)). In other words, learning communities can be a vehicle for addressing faculty issues such as lack of intellectual vitality, intellectual isolation, and inflexible reward systems.

In terms of professional networks between teacher educators and teachers, the evolving work on professional development schools provides models to inform the development of strategic plans, particularly with regard to bridging the gap between the knowledge acquired in teacher education programs and the application of that knowledge to performance in the classroom. The professional development school movement has many sources, but of special interest to this model is the Lab School that was so very common in early HBCUs. The teacher educator taught in both the college and the school, giving her the responsibility of providing a natural bridge between the knowledge imparted about teaching and the application of the demonstration of applications in the classroom. The teacher educator also models effective teaching strategies for the person in training. Since today's structures lend themselves better to partnerships between two persons, one from college and one from schools, we are more likely to approach the dual responsibilities for the pre-professional's knowledge and performance through partnerships between teachers and teacher educators. With evolving work on professional development schools, effective practices are developing, including 1) an emphasis on longer and more substantive clinical experiences, 2) teaching exchanges for college and school- based educators, and 3) joint research between teachers and teacher educators. The collaboration of university and school professionals can lead to the development of effective mechanisms for bridging the gap between knowledge and performance as well as between research and practice.

Developing Professional Foundations/ Coaching. In the coaching phase of the HBCUTSN model, attention is given to documentation and review of an institution's activities. Collaboration extends coaching to include information sharing. Potential areas for partnerships include the sharing of information within the institution, among HBCUs, and between teacher education units and P-12 schools. Two areas have already gained momentum. First are the case studies contained in this volume. These are vignettes of the collaborative efforts that have evolved through the implementation of various phases of the HBCUTSN model. The intent is to make information available to others, especially HBCUs, about effective strategies for enhancing teacher education programs. The second is the use of electronic databases for sharing information. In addition, more traditional services that might be considered include public forums, publications, and demonstration centers, all with a focus on effective collaboration strategies.

Beyond these, there will be other opportunities to provide services in response to specific needs. For example, there has been a call for colleges to provide services to school districts to help them implement changes mandated in legislation or in their own school or district plans. As noted at the outset, collaboration is a two-way process, driven by the needs of participants. Higher education institutions cannot make unilateral decisions about the needs of P-12 schools. For productive engagement, all participants must enter the relationship having clearly identified what they need and what they are giving to and receiving from the collaboration.

Using a strategic plan for collaboration, the unit can enhance its capacity 1) to identify and develop resources it may need from other sources in the education community; 2) to establish professional networks to promote improvement of teacher education programs; and 3) to serve as a resource for other higher education institutions and schools involved in improving the quality of education. In other words, during the collaborative phase of the technical assistance model, the institution is becoming adept at building an infrastructure for systemic change in three areas: resource development, clinical programs, and professional networking. In building an infrastructure, it is clearly not enough to point to fragments and pieces of the collaborative puzzle, addressing needs one by one. We need to look toward creating a vision of the "big picture"— not only where we want to go, but how we can get there. Further, schools and universities should be able to document and report the types of collaboratives that work well in addressing educational improvements. It follows then that in the future, the major goal of the collaborative component is to assist HBCUs in the development of strategic plans for collaboration in the areas of resource development, professional networking, and service development.

Guiding Principles for Developing Strategic Plans for Collaboration

Based on the experiences reported here, the network should consider five basic principles to guide future work with HBCUs in support of their development of Strategic Plans for Collaboration.

- **Strategic Plans for Collaboration must complement the strategic goals of the institution and the teacher education unit.**

It is important to make the strategic plans of the institution and the teacher education unit the focal point for the Strategic Plans for Collaboration. Typically, strategic plans describe long-term goals, usually five years, and short-term goals, which are annual targets or indicators for achieving incremental changes. We are confronted with the challenge of aligning the institutional strategic plan with those of its units. For example, the strategic plans for teacher education units must not only complement the institutional plan, but also reflect the requirements of accrediting agencies

- **Strategic Plans for Collaboration must provide for participants to be trained in effective strategies for engaging in collaboration.**

Some educational reform specialists have concluded that change from top-down and bottom-up must take place simultaneously (Fulan, 1987). A common viewpoint about the failure of a change effort is that members of collaboratives do not have knowledge of or practice with systematic problem solving, shared planning, or shared responsibilities — elements that make for effective collaboration

- **Strategic Plans for Collaboration must allow for the involvement of key partners in the development and implementation of the strategic plan.**

If strategic plans for collaboration are to be successful, consideration must be given to the needs of the teacher education unit as they relate to the strategic goals of the teacher education unit and the institution. The institution must know clearly how it, as a whole, will benefit from collaborative efforts of teacher education and other units. Further, we must acknowledge that benefits derived will involve other units on campus.

- **Strategic Plans for Collaboration must give consideration to collaboratives both within the institution and between the institution and external groups.**

Discussions of collaboratives tend to focus on partnerships between universities or schools and external constituents. Far less attention is given to partnerships within the institution, resulting in the failure to see many opportunities for maximizing existing resources and the tendency to give more attention to partnerships with external agencies.. .

- In the interest of systemic change, **Strategic Plans for Collaboration will actively seek ways and means of integrating related functions across units.**

This means accepting from the outset the possibility that reengineering or restructuring may evolve as the most reasonable way to address some problems. Such redesign may take formal avenues (restructured departments), transitional approaches (reassignment of faculty time within existing structures), or informal routes (cross-collaboration among faculty and students).

On a final note, it cannot be overemphasized that the present and future intent of the HBCU/TSN model is to provide the type of technical support that will enhance the overall effectiveness of teacher education units. This volume provides evidence that the Network has been beneficial. Future directions will likely include the development of Strategic Plans for Collaboration, with a view toward HBCUs continuing to meet the challenges of preserving their long tradition of educating teachers.

REFERENCES

Barth, Roland. (1996, Spring) School and university: Bad dreams, good dreams. *On Common Ground: Strengthening Teaching through School-University Partnership, 6*

Fullan, Michael. (1993) Innovation, reform, and restructuring strategies. Gordon Cawetti (ed.) In *Challenges and Achievements of American Education,* Alexandria, VA, Association for Supervision and Curriculum Development

Gablenick, Faite, Jean MacGregor, Roberta Matthews, and Barbara Leigh Smith. (1990, Spring) Learning communities: Creating connections among students, faculty, and disciplines. In *New Directions for Teaching and Learning,* 41. San Francisco: Jossey Bass

Goodlad, John, I. (1984) *A place called school*; New York: McGraw-Hill.

NCATE (1995) *Historically Black Colleges and Universities Teacher Education Technical Support Network Draft Manual*, Washington, D.C.

Robinson, Jay. (1996, Spring) University-school collaboration and educational reform. On Common Ground: *Strengthening Teaching through School-University Partnership, 6*

ABOUT THE
AUTHORS/CONTRIBUTORS

Loren J. Blanchard is a tenured assistant professor and educational psychologist in the Division of Education at Xavier University of Louisiana. He is the former chair of the division and recently served as its NCATE Coordinator. His research interest has centered on educating African-American male students. Blanchard is currently compiling a book of letters and journal entries on love and life experiences by African-American men.

Sister Doris Blum, S.B.S., is a professor of education in the Division of Education at Xavier University of Louisiana. She has served for 39 years at Xavier and initiated the Mild/Moderate Degree Special Education Program at Xavier. Blum is a Registered Music Therapist and has worked with special educators in using music to develop academic, behavioral, and motor skills for children with disabilities.

Mary B. Conley is the assistant dean, School of Education and an assistant professor in the Department of Curriculum and Instruction at Howard University in Washington, D.C. Conley has extensive experience as a public school educator and administrator. Her research interests include recruiting and training minorities for teaching; school university collaboration and partnerships; and urban school systemic reform issues. Conley is currently a member of the NCATE Board of Examiners.

JoAnne Smart Drane holds degrees from the University of North Carolina at Greensboro and from Duke University, Durham, North Carolina. Her professional experiences have spanned elementary, secondary, and higher education. She has been a guidance counselor, psychometrist, visiting instructor, local education administrator in various capacities including programs for exceptional children and federal programs, and special assistant to the superintendent. Most recently, she served as a consultant in teacher education and program approval for the North Carolina Department of Public Instruction. She is a member of the NCATE Board of Examiners.

Tommy L. Frederick earned the doctorate in Health Sciences from Indiana University in 1972. He is currently employed as acting dean, College of Arts and Sciences, at Delaware State University. Frederick is a member of the Governor's Coalition on Active Lifestyles and Fitness. He served on the Delaware Lung Association Board of Directors for several years. He published several textbooks in testing, research and wellness.

Cynthia J. Graddy is the executive assistant to the president of the American Association of Colleges for Teacher Education, where she provides coordination for work of the Board of Directors and Executive Office. She was previously a senior program associate in the Professional Issues Department at AACTE, where she provided oversight of conferences, publications, and accreditation issues. She also served as the central communications hub for HBCU/TSN institutions and consultant, including the Network's newsletter.

Delores R. Greene served her profession as a classroom teacher at all levels, a music teacher, a reading teacher, a director of Title IV, a director of Curriculum and Instruction, and an assistant superintendent for Elementary Education. She also has been a member of the Executive Council for the Association for Supervision and Curriculum Development and co-founder of its African American Critical Issues Network. She is currently chair of the Department of Teacher Education and Interdisciplinary Studies at Virginia Union University in Richmond, Virginia.

Aleta Hannah is a veteran educator who is an assistant professor at Delaware State University. She chairs the Department of Education which is composed of six undergraduate and four graduate programs, chairs the Teacher Education Council and the Teaching Effectiveness Committee, co-leads the NCATE Steering Team, and participates in numerous other university committees. She also serves on many state committees that have an impact on the direction of education.

B. Denise Hawkins is an assistant vice president at The Widmeyer-Baker Group, Inc. in Washington, D.C. She also works as a freelance print journalist. She is a former news editor and senior writer at Black Issues in Higher Education magazine where she covered HBCU's and legal education. Ms. Hawkins is also a former medical writer for the Army Times News Service and a news director for the United Methodist News Service. She earned her undergraduate degree from Howard University and her master's degree from The Pennsylvania State University.

Kay L. Hegler is professor of education and assessment officer at Doane College, in Crete, Nebraska. She teaches Special Education, qualitative research, and multiculturalism. Her work for program improvement is implemented through NCATE as a member of the BoE and the HBCU-TSN. She leads Doane's NCA general education assessment efforts. She is a member of the Board of Directors, the Nebraska Network for Educational Renewal.

Charles M. Hodge is associate provost and graduate dean, Bowie State University. Combining theory with practice, he has initiated a broad spectrum of reforms in teacher education. A strong advocate of the collaborative approach to schooling and educator preparation, Hodge's research interests include higher education governance, and equity and diversity among and within educational institutions. His writings appear in several professional journals.

David G. Imig is president and chief executive officer of the American Association of Colleges for Teacher Education. A leader in national and international teacher education policy and professional practice issues, he serves on the boards of numerous associations and education projects.

George Robert Johnson Jr., the ninth president of LeMoyne-Owen College, is the former associate dean and professor, Howard University

School of Law; former assistant general counsel, Executive Office of the President, White House Council on Wage and Price Stability; and former assistant counsel, Committee on Banking, Finance and Urban Affairs, U.S. House of Representatives. Previously he also taught at George Mason University, School of Law, in Arlington, Virginia. He has published in the George Mason Law Review, the Administrative Law Review and the Harvard Environmental Law Review. He also is a contributor to the African-American Almanac and the editor of Popular Sovereignty: The Will of the People.

Fannye E. Love is an associate professor of Elementary Education and coordinator of Graduate Programs at the University of Mississippi. She has worked as a classroom teacher, reading supervisor/specialist, assistant professor and chairperson of teacher education. She received her B.S. degree from Mississippi Valley State University, her M. Ed. in reading, and her Ph.D. in Curriculum and Instruction from the University of Mississippi. She has authored articles and presented at conferences in the areas of reading and early childhood education. She is currently a member of the NCATE Board of Examiners.

Sister Angela T. Lydon is a tenured professor of education at Xavier University of Louisiana. She teaches graduate courses and works with administrators and teachers in urban elementary schools to envision new and dynamic curricular approaches. These curricular approaches are integrative, earth-centered, and reflective of student diversity.

Donna Jones Miles is assistant professor in the Teacher Education Department at Virginia Union University in Richmond, Virginia. She is the sponsor for the campus Student Education Association and a chair of the self-study Steering Committee for SACS. Also, she is the newly elected Secretary-Treasurer for the Virginia Association of Colleges for Teacher Education.

Andrea L. Miller is vice president for academic affairs/dean of faculty and professor of Biology at LeMoyne-Owen College in Memphis, Tennessee. She serves as a consultant to local high schools in the areas of student outcomes assessment, organizational development, institutional effectiveness and strategic planning. Miller is currently collaborating on the development of a book that analyzes the viewpoints, experiences, and challenges of selected White faculty members at Historically Black Colleges and Universities.

Glennie H. Mueller is coordinator of Field-Based Instruction and an instructor in Teacher Education at Virginia Union University in Richmond, Virginia. She facilitates collaboration with metropolitan area schools for course field placement and student teaching. She also is responsible for graduate follow-up. Her teaching focus is in curriculum and instruction as well as reading.

Alex Poinsett, a Chicago freelance journalist, authored the political biography, Walking With Presidents: Louis Martin and Rise of Black Political Power, published in May 1997 under auspices of the Washington, D.C.-based Joint Center for Political and Economic Studies. The former Ebony Magazine editor also has been a consultant on social, political, and educational affairs for the Carnegie Corporation of New York and the Ford Foundation.

Sharon Robinson is the senior vice president and chief operating officer for the Educational Testing Service. From 1993 through 1996, she served as the assistant secretary for the Office of Educational Research and Improvement in the U.S. Department of Education. Prior to 1993, Robinson was the director of the National Center for Innovation at the National Education Association.

Jerrie Cobb Scott is a linguist and educator researcher. She is currently professor of education and was formerly director of the Office of Diversity at the University of Memphis and Dean of Education at Central State University of Ohio. She has served as a consultant for educational programs in the areas of accreditation preparation, classroom, institutional and workforce diversity, literacy development, and business, community, university and school collaboratives. In these areas, she has published extensively. Scott also is founder and national director of the African-American Read-In Chain, a literacy promotion that began in 1989.

Carol E. Smith is senior director for Professional Issues at the American Association of Colleges for Teacher Education, where she serves as NCATE liaison and coordinates professional standards and assessment issues. She also works with technical assistance to teacher education programs and served as assistant project director for the Historically Black Colleges and Universities Technical Support Network.

Veronica G. Thomas is the interim dean, School of Education and a professor in the Department of Human Development and Psychoeducational Studies at Howard University. Her research interests include mid-life development, gender roles, the psychology of African-American women, well-being and coping in families, and career aspirations of adolescents. As a trained social psychologist, Thomas has published numerous articles, book chapters, and monographs. Her work has appeared in journals such as Women and Health and the Journal of the National Medical Association.

Johnny E. Tolliver earned his Ph.D. at Harvard University. He is the provost and vice president for academic affairs, and professor of English, at Delaware State University in Dover, Delaware. He also is chief operating officer and chief academic officer for Delaware State University, second-in-command to the president. Tolliver is responsible for the day-to-day operation of the university and the Division of Academic Affairs. He manages an operating budget of $50 million.

Gwendolyn Trotter, currently dean of Education at Butler University in Indianapolis, Indiana, conceptualized the HBCU Technical Support Framework. This conceptualization took place through experiences at Grambling State University, Tuskegee, North Carolina A&T, and Florida A&M University. Trotter also serves on several committees for the American Association of Colleges for Teacher Education and the Association of Teacher Educators (ATE), and is currently a member of the NCATE Board of Examiners.

Margaret Cole White, currently interim director of Teacher Education at Elizabeth City State University, has worked extensively in the public schools in various capacities. White has continued to work with colleges and universities preparing to obtain national accreditation. Her most recent continuing work has been as a lead consultant (process-product developer and trainer) for the Historically Black Colleges and Universities Technical Support Network (HBCUTSN), and is currently a member of the NCATE Board of Examiners.

Boyce C. Williams is vice president, Institutional Relations, at the National Council for Accreditation of Teacher Education. She works closely with institutions to help implement the accreditation process smoothly and efficiently. She has authored articles on diversity and collaboration in teacher education, most recently having served as a guest editor for the Association of Teacher Education Journal. Williams was conferred an Honorary Doctorate for Public Service and Leadership at Cheyney University and received the Honorary Doctorate of Humane Letters degree from Virginia Union University. She also is an NCATE/NBPTS collaborator.

Darnell Williams is the director of the Langston University Center for International Development (LUCID) and teaches graduate courses in English as a Second Language and Bilingual/Multicultural Education. He has taught at Ohio State University and Bishop College, as well as in the public school systems in Indiana and Texas. He has been involved in multicultural education, including bilingual education and English as a Second Language for 33 years. He received the Bachelor of Science Degree in Spanish and French from Bishop College, the Master of Arts Degree in Spanish from Ohio State University, the Specialist Certification in English as a Second Language from Ohio State University, and the Doctor of Philosophy Degree in English Education from Ohio State University. Williams also currently serves as a member of NCATE's Board of Examiners.

Arthur E. Wise is president of the National Council for Accreditation of Teacher Education (NCATE) in Washington, D.C. At NCATE, he has directed the implementation of its rigorous standards and procedures, and initiated efforts to develop a system of quality assurance for the teaching profession. Wise is formerly director of the Rand Corporation. He is widely known for Rich Schools/Poor Schools.

Doris E. Wooledge earned the Ed.D. from University of Missouri-Columbia. She is employed as acting chairperson, Department of Health and Human Performance, at Delaware State University. Wooledge serves as a national NCATE/NASPE program reviewer; serves on the Regional Council for Conventions for Health, Physical Education, Recreation and Dance, Eastern District; and serves on the Governor's Coalition for Active Lifestyles and Fitness. She has published several articles.

HBCU Technical Support Network Project

Acknowledgements are extended to the following for their roles in the conception, development, and implementation of the technical support network.

Presidential Task Force

**Lloyd Vic Hackley, Immediate Past President,
Fayetteville State University**

**Jimmy R. Jenkins, President,
Edward Waters College**

Burnett Joiner, President, LeMoyne-Owen College

**Joel Nwagbaroacha, Past President,
Barber-Scotia College**

Talbert Shaw, President, Shaw University

**Mary Smith, Immediate Past President,
Kentucky State University**

Myer L. Titus, President, Philander-Smith College

Ex Officio Task Force

**Sam Cargile, DeWitt Wallace Reader's Digest Fund
Kent McGuire, Assistant Secretary,
Office of Educational Research and Improvement**

Technical Consultants

**Pauletta Brown Bracy,
North Carolina Central University**

Mary B. Conley, Howard University

Loretta Davenport, LeMoyne-Owen College

JoAnne Smart Drane, Raleigh,
North Carolina

Beverly Downing, Saint Augustine's College

Rose Duhon-Sells, McNeese State University

Dwight Fennell, Paul Quinn College

Marian Gillis-Olion, Fayetteville State University

Kay Hegler, Doane College

Charles M. Hodge, Bowie State University

Thomas Jackson, Tallahassee, Florida

Paul Mehta, Prairie View A&M University

Dorothy Prince-Barnett,
Greensboro, North Carolina

Leroy Simmons, Florida A&M University

Diane Simon, Virginia Commonwealth University

Gwendolyn Trotter, Butler University

Lelia Vickers, Winston-Salem State University

Albert Walker, Elizabeth City State University

Margaret Cole White,
Elizabeth City State University

Darnell Williams, Langston University

Shirley Winstead, Norfolk State University

Elaine P. Witty, Norfolk State University

Adjunct Consultants

Mary E. Diez, Alverno College

Richard Dudley, Doane College

Gary R. Galluzzo, George Mason University

B. Denise Hawkins, Clifton, Virginia

Fannye Love, University of Mississippi

Alex Poinsett, Chicago, Illinois

Lilburn E. Wesche, Boise, Idaho